To Paul:
May we all work
12 steps on everything.
Best, Frank L.

THE 12 STEPS FOR EVERYBODY

A 12-Step Program for Those Who Wish
To Work the 12 Steps on Anything

FIFTH EDITION

THE 12 STEPS FOR EVERYBODY, INC.
Pacific Palisades
2007

The 12 Steps for Everybody, Inc.; the book, "The 12 Steps for Everybody"; and all of the T.S.E. 12-Step materials are based on the 12-Step program of Alcoholics Anonymous. The Twelve Steps have been adapted and reprinted with permission of Alcoholics Anonymous World Services, Inc. However, the writings and opinions on this material are those of the authors only and not of Alcoholics Anonymous.

For inquiries, orders, and requests write to:

The 12 Steps for Everybody, Inc.
P.O. Box 444
Pacific Palisades, CA 90272
Telephone: 310-428-0904
E-Mail: info@12stepsforeverybody.org
Website: www.12stepsforeverybody.org

The 12 Steps for Everybody is a California 501(c)(3) nonprofit corporation whose mission is to provide free information, literature, 12-Step meetings, 12-Step workshops, and personal support to all those who wish to work the 12 Steps on anything. Donations will be gratefully accepted and are tax deductible. Tax I.D. No. 20-3809570.

Library of Congress Control No. 2007923742
ISBN 978-1-4243-3456-8
Manufactured in the United States of America

CONTENTS

PREFACE

The idea for The 12 Steps for Everybody arose while attending various 12-Step programs from 1979 to 1987, including A.A., A.C.A., Al-Anon, D.A., E.A., G.A., O.A., and S.A. Some of us could see that not only could the 12 Steps of Alcoholics Anonymous be applied to addictions other than alcohol, but they could also be applied to various mental and emotional problems, and even to various so-called defects of character, shortcomings, or maladaptive behaviors.

In 1988, we self-published the first book entitled "The 12 Steps for Everybody," formed a State of California for-profit corporation with the same name, and started a 12 Steps for Everybody discussion meeting at a church in South Miami, Florida. The meeting lasted for six months and then died off for lack of interest.

In 1989, we re-published the book, "The 12 Steps for Everybody" and started a 12 Steps for Everybody discussion meeting in West Los Angeles, California. The meeting lasted for one year and also died off for lack of interest. The for-profit corporation was dissolved in 1990, due to lack of funding, and the third edition of the book was published and distributed free of charge to anyone who requested it. In 1992, a fourth edition of the book was published and has been distributed free of charge up to the present.

In 2005, we became inspired to start a 12 Steps for Everybody writing meeting/workshop at the SHARE! (Self-Help And Recovery Exchange) center in Mar Vista, California with the format as described in "Appendix III." At that time our contention was that 12-Step discussion meetings do not seem to have the power of insight and recovery that 12-Step writing meetings or workshops have.

In October 2005, a State of California charitable nonprofit corporation for the public benefit named "The 12 Steps for

Everybody" (T.S.E.) was formed with the mission to provide free information, literature, 12-Step meetings, 12-Step writing workshops, and personal support to anyone wishing to work the 12 Steps on anything.

So far, the TSE materials include this fifth edition of the book; the website: www.12stepsforeverybody.org; the meeting format, 12 Steps, and 12 Traditions described in "Appendix III"; the 12-Step writing workshop questions described in "Appendix IV"; and various sets of 12-Step writing worksheets that are used in ongoing 12-Step writing meetings and workshops. (See the website at www.12stepsforeverybody.org for more information.)

The 12 Steps for Everybody is not meant to supplant other existing and ongoing 12-Step programs or self-help support groups. Our mission is to help all those who wish to work the 12 Steps on any addiction, obsession-compulsion, mental and emotional problem, chronic illness and disability, or any other habitual problem in their lives.

If you have any questions about working the 12 Steps or anything else in the above, write to: *The 12 Steps for Everybody, P.O. Box 444, Pacific Palisades, CA 90272; call 310-428-0904, e-mail info@12stepsforeverybody.org; or visit www.12stepsforeverybody.org.*

FOREWORD

"As We Understood God"

Many people have a problem with the word "God," or the various concepts or connotations the word carries. Some were raised with a strict religious upbringing and resent the ideas and demands presented to them. Still others had no religious upbringing at all or were taught that there is no God and that all life begins and ends at birth and death.

Many feel that if there is a God, He must be cruel and unusual to create such a cruel and unusual universe. Still others have pondered the question of God until it has driven them to a state of abject confusion.

The 12 Steps for Everybody does not wish to foist any concepts or beliefs about God onto anyone. We use the word "God" in a *general* sense to mean any concept of a "Higher Power" that you may have, even if it is nothing more than the collective love and good will of two or more people sharing their experience, strength, and hope with each other.

Interestingly enough, many people have been staying sober in Alcoholics Anonymous for many years by using the "AA group" as their Higher Power. Others have used "nature," "the ocean," or what they call their "higher self" – their conscience. Some even merely use "the spiritual principles" as a higher power. The spiritual principles, as we understand them, include: gratitude, humility, honesty, purity, unselfishness, love, patience, tolerance, compassion, understanding, acceptance, forgiveness, faith, hope, and charity (service).

In fact, you don't have to believe in God to practice the spiritual principles. They are intrinsic to Step 12, and when we apply these spiritual principles to our daily lives and to the people and situations around us, we experience recovery, peace, and joy. The spiritual principles themselves have a healing power that transcends anything we medically understand.

So, for those of you who have trouble believing in God, remember that you can experience relief from your addiction, obsession-compulsion, or habitual problem by simply working Steps 1 and 12. We call it "two-stepping." All you have to do is to recognize that you are powerless over whatever it is that is troubling you, that your life becomes unmanageable when you allow the problem to trouble you, and that by practicing spiritual principles in your life you can experience some measure of recovery.

If you have any questions about working the 12 Steps or anything else in the above, write to: *The 12 Steps for Everybody, P.O. Box 444, Pacific Palisades, CA 90272; call 310-428-0904, e-mail info@12stepsforeverybody.org; or visit www.12stepsforeverybody.org.*

THE 12 STEPS FOR EVERYBODY

THE DOCTOR'S OPINION

To Whom It May Concern:

I have been a licensed psychotherapist in the State of California for ten years, specializing in the treatment of marriage and family problems, substance abuse, chronic illness and disability, and problems with aging. During this time I have observed that clients who regularly attend 12-Step programs, whatever their addiction or chronic problem, do much better in psychotherapeutic counseling, and consequently tend to do much better in their recovery.

It is estimated there are over 500 self-help support groups throughout the world today. While most of these programs focus on recovery from one individualized addiction, obsessive-compulsion, or psychoneurotic illness, The 12 Steps for Everybody (T.S.E.), based on the original program of Alcoholics Anonymous, opens its doors to the treatment of *any* or *all* habitual problems.

I first became acquainted with T.S.E. in 1990, when I witnessed a man using the 12-Steps to deal with degenerative arthritis and chronic back pain. Subsequently, I saw him apply the 12 Steps to excessive anger, free-floating anxiety, agitated depression, paranoia, and low self-esteem. While he was attending other 12-Step programs at the time, T.S.E. acted as a valuable adjunct in focusing his attention on the particular symptom that was bothering him in the moment, and in emphasizing the *sustained action* of working the 12 Steps in a *continuous* effort.

The curative powers of the 12 Steps lie in their intrinsic two-pronged approach – behavior modification and spiritual action. The T.S.E. 12-Step writing meetings and workshops to which I refer my patients are a particularly powerful method of applying the 12 Steps, because they give people the freedom to focus and write on *whatever* problem or symptom happens to be bothering them at the time. During the writing and sharing process, seemingly baffling habitual problems become more concrete and less overwhelming. The apparently infinite problem becomes finite, and one can then prioritize its negative aspects and work the applicable Steps to let go of it.

Participants in T.S.E. 12-Step writing meetings and workshops are given the choice to share or not to share what they have written, which gives them a sense of latitude and autonomy in their recovery. However, if they choose to share their writing out loud, the benefits are threefold. The participants contribute and receive a variety of ways of dealing with their problem; they receive the spiritual and therapeutic lift of practicing empathy and nonjudgment, while listening to the problems of others; and they can take the insights and solutions they have learned to their sponsor or therapist to develop a treatment plan that is satisfactory to both. Thus, the individual becomes an expert in the resolution of his or her own problem.

For those who are members of other 12-Step programs or self-help support groups, for those who have multiple addictions or obsessive-compulsive behaviors, and for those whose only problem is a bothersome habit they would like to overcome, I highly recommend involvement in The 12 Steps for Everybody.

Linda M. Lawson, L.M.F.T., Psy.D.

INTRODUCTION

One morning in August of 1977, I tried to push my second ex-wife out of a moving car going 50 m.p.h. We were coming from my psychiatrist's office and I remember the incident quite well, because at the time it occurred to me that we might not be going fast enough to kill her. She'll probably only get maimed or crippled, I thought, and then I'll have *that* on my conscience! I can't win! Nothing I *do* seems to work out right anymore!

I was completely out of control at the time, stoned on Thorazine and marijuana at 11:00 a.m., shouting, crying, unemployable, convinced my wife was cheating on me and totally dependent on her every move. Late at night I would put little stones on the tops of her car wheels, so that I could check in the morning to see if she had snuck out while I was asleep. When she came home from a trip to the store, I would sniff her to see if I could detect any suspicious odors. It's sad when you think about it, that a person could become that obsessed over the actions of another human being. Anybody out there identify?

What are we talking about here? Drug addiction, jealousy, paranoia? What was going on with me? Was I suffering some strange psychoneurotic disease brought on by genetics, hormonal imbalance, or early traumatic conditioning? Was I in the throes of a diabetic coma or a pre-epileptic seizure? What ungodly quirk in my character caused me to mentally, emotionally, and physically abuse the very person in my life whom I loved the most, i.e., my second ex-wife?

Today I have come to realize that the basis of my insanity over my second ex-wife was an "obsession-compulsion" called *codependence*, an addiction so powerful that it ruined my life in all areas, and one of the many addictions I have suffered over the years. In fact, today I have come to believe that *all* irrational behaviors that are done repeatedly, over and over, can be called *addictions*.

What is codependence, or for that matter, what is addiction? There are many definitions – "being out of control or under the control of some person, place, or thing;" "tending to perform a certain act over and over in a certain way;" "irresistibly compelled to behave in an irrational manner."

There are as many different definitions of addiction as there are dictionaries and the experts who write them. The point is, it doesn't really matter what the definition is. With addictions it doesn't even *matter* where they originate. In fact, one of the characteristics of addictions is that we try to understand them in order to get rid of them, and that never really works.

Addictions are "cunning, baffling, and powerful," as one 12-Step program describes them. You can sit up all hours of the night, trying to figure out who or what is the cause of that compulsion you have to eat a dozen donuts, or to obsess over your ex-lover, or to think negative thoughts about yourself; but when it gets right down to the nitty-gritty with addictions, trying to figure them out is like a dog chasing its tail. You're never going to catch it. And just when you think you do, it slips away, and there it is again, wagging at you.

I'll give you an example. One of my habits is taking off my glasses, looking through them to see if they're dirty, cleaning them with my pocket-handkerchief, and then putting them back on again. I used to do it at least two or three times a day. When I was younger, I would do it maybe ten or fifteen times a day. In fact, as I grew to realize where it came from (that this was what my father used to do, so I was unconsciously modeling my father's behavior), I experienced an initial relief and some remission from this "insignificant" little addiction.

However, now I am seventy years-old and guess what I find myself doing once in a while, without even thinking about it, during the day when I am under a little stress? Taking off my glasses, looking through them to see if they are dirty, cleaning them with my pocket-handkerchief, and then putting them back on again! *Understanding* where it comes from doesn't take it away.

Checking your glasses is a rather harmless little addiction. Not like alcoholism, guilt, or *doormatism* (the need to be treated like a doormat). I guess I haven't reached my "bottom" yet on checking my glasses. Maybe I never will. The pain, or *negative consequences*, of the act of checking my glasses haven't gotten great enough to motivate me to quit. It is my opinion that addictions are not always bad.

There are probably some good addictions. Being "on time" is one of mine. Other people seem to appreciate it when I'm on time. My employers certainly do. My two ex-wives certainly didn't, because I was always bugging them to hurry up, and they didn't have my compulsion to be on time. So sometimes our addictions can conflict with the lives of others, despite the fact that they are "good" in our own eyes.

But to get back to my second ex-wife and codependence as an addiction. Some people (such as myself) were raised in alcoholic and/or dysfunctional families, and we have certain traits we have picked up along the way. Some of these include chronic shame, guilt, fear, rage, self-destructiveness, feelings of not belonging (alienation), the tendency to stuff our feelings, addiction to helping others, addiction to damaged people (and relationships), and over-achievement, just to name a few.

These traits, or aspects of our character, have become "addictions" in their own right; and we find ourselves unable to stop practicing them, despite the fact that they are destroying our lives. Because of my addiction to (and dependence on) my second ex-wife and the symbiotic codependent love I had for her, I would have rather pushed her out of a moving car going 50 m.p.h. than to have lived without her meeting my expectations. Makes sense, doesn't it? Sort of like, "I love you so much I'll *kill* you, if you don't do what I want you to do."

But codependence is only one of literally hundreds of addictions from which we can suffer. The catch is, for all practical purposes, only *you* can say what your addictions are and what you want to do about them. Because if you *do* want to do something about them, there is a way to alleviate them. And that way is to work the 12 Steps of one or more of the 12-Step programs. Off hand, I count nineteen 12-Step programs for which I qualify:

A.A.: Alcoholics Anonymous
A.C.A.: Adult Children of Alcoholics
(and Dysfunctional Families)
Al-Anon: for family members of alcoholics
C.A.: Cocaine Anonymous
Co-Anon: for family members of cocaine addicts
CoDA: Co-Dependents Anonymous
D.A.: Debtors Anonymous
E.A.: Emotions Anonymous
E.H.A.: Emotional Health Anonymous
F.A.: Families Anonymous
G.A.: Gamblers Anonymous
M.A.: Marijuana Anonymous
N.A.: Narcotics Anonymous
N.A.: Nicotine Anonymous
O.A.: Overeaters Anonymous
P.A.: Parents Anonymous
S.A.: Sexaholics Anonymous
S.L.A.A.: Sex and Love Addicts Anonymous
S.A.: Smokers Anonymous

I know that today there are many others for which I could identify. Today, I regularly attend two of the 12-Step meetings above, and I try to work the 12 Steps of the other seventeen whenever possible. I also started a 12-Step program called "The 12 Steps for Everybody" in 1988, whose purpose it is to work the 12 Steps on *anything*. I'm probably the "World's Most Addicted Person." But where did all of these 12-Step programs come from originally?

In June 1935, a New York stockbroker named Bill W. and an Akron physician named Bob S. (Dr. Bob) discovered that together they could do what neither was able to do alone, that is, stay sober from alcohol. Of course, for a non-alcoholic the simple act of refraining from alcohol is child's play; but to those two booze-fighting, two-fisted, morning-after middle-aged guys, *not* taking a drink had been out of the question for twenty-five years.

It was so impossible for either of those two men *not* to drink (as it has been for millions of alcoholics down through the ages) that their addiction to alcohol had almost totally ruined their lives. Their marriages were barely intact. They had both become occupationally dysfunctional. And both were suffering complete financial destitution and social disrepute. Not bad for two well-bred, college-educated professional people!

And yet in the course of one evening's conversation, both of these creators of the parent 12-Step program, Alcoholics Anonymous, discovered the secret not only to staying sober from their addiction to alcohol, but also to turning their lives around and becoming happy, useful members of society once again. That secret is contained in working the *12 Steps*, or spiritual practices, that evolved in the early formative years of Alcoholics Anonymous. They are listed below.

THE 12 STEPS

1. We admitted we were powerless over alcohol – that our lives had become unmanageable.

2. Came to believe that a Power greater than ourselves could restore us to sanity.

3. Made a decision to turn our will and our lives over to the care of God as we understood God.

4. Made a searching and fearless moral inventory of ourselves.

5. Admitted to God, to ourselves, and to another human being the exact nature of our wrongs.

6. Were entirely ready to have God remove all these defects of character.

7. Humbly asked God to remove our shortcomings.

8. Made a list of all persons we had harmed, and became willing to make amends to them all.

9. Made direct amends to such people wherever possible, except when to do so would injure them or others.

10. Continued to take personal inventory and when we were wrong promptly admitted it.

11. Sought through prayer and meditation to improve our conscious contact with God as we understood God, praying only for knowledge of His will for us and the power to

carry that out.

12. Having had a spiritual awakening as the result of these steps, we tried to carry this message to alcoholics, and to practice these principles in all our affairs.

(The 12 Steps are reprinted and adapted with permission of Alcoholics Anonymous World Services, Inc. The opinions on this material are those of the authors only and not of A.A.)

After the two alcoholics, Bill and Bob, invented the 12 Steps, it was discovered that the family members of alcoholics could get just as sick as the alcoholics themselves, and so the program of Al-Anon was developed by merely changing *one* word in the 12th Step – "alcoholics" to "others." It was also discovered that the same kind of physical, mental, emotional, and spiritual destitution was possible abusing other addictions besides alcohol.

And so it is possible to work the 12 Steps on *anything* you feel you are addicted to, *anything* in your life you would like to change, or any *irrational behavior* that you tend to practice repeatedly. The rest of the 12-Step programs have followed suit by simply changing the word *alcohol* in the 1st Step to *whatever* applies – narcotics, food, gambling, emotions, television, and so forth.

We live in an addictive society. Everywhere you turn you see people addicted to work, money, life in the fast lane (speeding, gobbling down food, running around like chickens with their heads cut off). There are sugar addicts, movie addicts, and telephone addicts. Enough is never enough for an addict, and just *one* always leads to *just one more*, whether it's a cup of coffee, a television show, or a potato chip.

If any of this makes any sense to you, or sounds even vaguely familiar to your life, you may be a candidate for this book and working the 12 Steps on some habitual problematic aspect of your life or your personality. I believe the most insidious habits we can experience are what I label the *intangible* addictions (irrational behaviors) like anxiety, depression, guilt, paranoia, and obsession.

When you lie awake for hours at night, running the same tape loops in your brain, over and over again, you begin to know what obsession is all about and just how helpless you can feel struggling with it. And yet the addiction to obsession can be overcome and released by the consistent application of the 12 Steps.

Of course, it sounds simple, but it is not easy. First, you have to reach a painful *bottom* on your addiction, a point where you become "sick and tired of being sick and tired" of whatever it is you are addicted to. Then, you must become willing to admit your powerlessness and to surrender and let go. Self-discovery, self-disclosure, and forgiveness are integral aspects of the 12 Steps, as are acceptance, amends, meditation, and working with others.

The 12 Steps are for those who have tried everything else. They are the last resort for the confrontation of, overcoming of, and release from addictions and irrational behaviors that have defied all other strategies. They are what succeeds after the denial has been broken, the blame has been worn out, and the feelings have been exposed and explored ad infinitum.

This book is about my experience with over twenty-five separate addictions, many of which gave me so much pain I often prayed to die just to escape the suffering. I tell how I identified the addictions, how they affected my life, how I reached my bottom, and how I finally became willing and able to let go of them. I also write about how I continue to work the 12 Steps on my addictions and the many positive benefits I derive from letting go of those addictions.

The opinions in this book are my own and may not reflect

those of any other 12-Step programs or members. Here I share my experience, strength, and hope on the 12 Steps with you, so that someday you may experience the same serenity and joy I have in my life today, and someday you may pass it on.

Chapter 1

ALCOHOL & DRUGS

I was born in 1936, into an upper-middle class suburban family on the East coast. Although both my parents came from poor backgrounds, my father had worked his way up to becoming president and chairman of the board of a large corporation, despite his frequent heavy drinking. My mother was a homemaker and played golf and bridge at the local country club.

From my earliest childhood I felt as if I came from another planet. I often asked my parents if I was adopted, because I certainly didn't feel like I belonged in that family. In fact, every place I ever went I always felt as though I should be some place else.

Yet I always managed to make a good showing of myself. I was an excellent student in the private school I attended, and I played on all the athletic teams and won awards at all the summer camps. In any early photograph, you're sure to see me with a strained smile on my face. I was a great actor. But deep down I was dying inside with fear, depression, and guilt. For what, I did not know.

Some of the most exciting times in my childhood were the countless cocktail parties at the yacht clubs, country clubs, and private homes of my parents and their friends. Out in the kitchen, the men would pour me little shots of straight whiskey, and I would try to take them down without flinching. Even then I enjoyed playing the hero.

Later, when no one was looking, I would wander through the party, drinking the unfinished drinks I would find on tables, stairs, and mantle pieces. It gave me a warm, glowing, superior feeling. My shyness would drop away, and I would vie to be the center of attention, although without booze I was very self-conscious and withdrawn.

By the time I was fifteen, I was a weekend drunk. My school friends and I bought pints of whiskey and six-packs of beer on Friday and Saturday nights and went around the city, crashing parties and trying to pick up girls. On Sunday, I would sleep it off and try to get in shape to go back to school on Monday.

My grades and my athletic prowess went downhill fast, and at the age of seventeen I had a nervous breakdown and was locked up in a mental institution for six months with "psychoneurosis and obsessive-compulsive tendencies." I thought there was a "plot" and that everybody around me was a paid actor, paid to check up on me and carry the information back to a "master scientist." I thought I was dying of cancer. And I thought my mother was trying to kill me by poisoning the sugar bowl.

I learned a lot about my psychological condition in the mental institution, and I managed to stay off alcohol for six whole months while I was locked up. But that didn't stop me from going right back to drinking again as soon as I got out. What this shows me about addictions, in general, is that understanding *why* you indulge in a certain habit doesn't stop you from continuing to indulge in that habit.

In fact, over the next twenty-five years of alcoholic drinking, I was to go to six different psychiatrists for psychotherapy and intensive psychoanalysis; and no amount of insight or understanding into the causes of my addiction to alcohol, drugs, cigarettes, coffee, sugar, sex, or whatever else, enabled me to stop. When the addict craves a fix, nothing except the 12 Steps will stop the addict from getting that fix. This is my experience.

After the mental institution, there proceeded a long series of jobs, relationships, and "geographics" (physical moves from one place to another) before I finally decided, with nothing better to do, to join the Army at the age of twenty. I was sent to peacetime Korea, where my drinking and my addiction to gambling began to emerge in full force. I became involved in illegal activities in the Army and was lucky to get out, after some difficulty, with an honorable discharge.

Then there proceeded a long list of jobs, relationships, geographics, and attempts at college. I was never satisfied with where I was, who I was with, where I was working, or what I was doing; but mainly I wasn't satisfied with who *I was*. My self-esteem and my self-worth were zero. Unless I was high on something, I was always filled with anxiety and depression.

Guilt and paranoia were my constant companions. Resentment was my middle name. I honestly don't see how I survived those years before my first marriage, except that I always had my parents' home and money to fall back on, and I was incredibly lucky, if you want to call it that.

The year my parents both died (1962), I was twenty-six. They left me with an estate income that enabled me to drink for another sixteen years. My addiction to codependence (the need for someone else to feed and lean on) was so great that I married the first woman who would have me, and thus followed two eight-year marriages, complete with houses, furniture, cars, children, dogs, and a swimming pool.

Without going into detail, I lost them all to alcohol, drugs, and the various forms of insanity to which I had been addicted all my life. Suffice it to say that everyone else in my life, including myself, suffered as much or more than I did from my addictions.

When I came to my first 12-Step program at the age of forty-two, I was homeless, jobless, wifeless, $5000 in debt, and running up my twelve credit cards with the thought of skipping town and changing my identity. I was so strung out I couldn't get high on anything anymore. I was so paranoid I thought people in phone booths and football huddles were talking about me.

I was so filled with anxiety and depression I couldn't breathe. I wanted to die, and I didn't know how to pull it off. I guess you might say I had reached a pretty solid "bottom," when I went to my first 12-Step meeting on a Friday night in 1979 in a posh section of the town where I was living at the time.

The people were all wearing cashmere sweaters and gold chains, and they were all smiling. At first I thought it was some kind of put-on, maybe another "plot" just to make a fool out of me, or maybe some kind of weird surprise party. But when I heard the speakers at the meeting telling my story; how they, too, had felt isolated and alone; how their lives had gone from bad to worse; how the common denominator in all of their physical, mental, and emotional problems was the addiction to alcohol and drugs, I identified. I felt that I had finally come home!

Finally, there was a place where I was understood and people who understood me. And I understood them, how they felt, how they behaved, and how they had become so desperate. They were desperate enough to do anything to gain freedom from the bondage of their addiction.

At that very first 12-Step meeting I learned another important aspect of recovery from addictions, and that is, getting with people who have the same addiction you have. The identification with others of the same "breed" provides the necessary atmosphere for acceptance, mutual support, and unconditional love that is so important to the addict who is often just coming in from a world of *no* acceptance, *no* support, and maybe even *no* love. This is why attending the 12-Step meetings on a regular basis is so critical to early and ongoing recovery. We can do together what we cannot do alone.

Although it is not always the case with every alcoholic, I lost the obsession to drink alcohol and to use drugs at that very first 12-Step meeting. They told me to go to ninety meetings in ninety days, and I did exactly that. They shared their experience, strength, and hope, telling me what it was like when they were drinking, what happened to bring them to their first 12-Step meeting, and what it was like now that they were sober.

They told me to work the 12 Steps, and looking at the 12 Steps up on the wall, printed out on a white "window shade," I just couldn't imagine what those twelve sentences had to do with anything, much less giving up alcohol.

You have to realize I had tried *everything* to give up drinking for twenty-seven years, and drugs the last ten years of that, and nothing had enabled me to do it! No amount of will power, no paperback self-help books, no psychiatrists, no health programs, no solemn oaths, no threats, nothing had worked. And then along came these 12-Step people with their cheery faces and their "keep comin' backs," and all of a sudden I didn't even want to drink or use anymore. I didn't even *think* about it.

I could not understand the phenomenon of the 1st Step: "We admitted we were powerless over alcohol – that our lives had become unmanageable." I could not understand how admitting that you were powerless, that you had no control whatsoever over a thing, could thus enable you to *control* that thing. How could you get power from admitting you were powerless? It just didn't make any sense to me at the time. All of my academic training, my three college degrees, my teaching and business experience, told me that in order to have power you had to generate it and exercise it yourself. The idea of surrendering, giving up, was incomprehensible to me.

But the key to my giving up these two particular addictions at that particular time was the bottom I had reached on alcohol and drugs and my reaction to that bottom. I had lost everything in my own mind, and I was desperate enough over that fact at that moment to do something about it. I was desperate enough to do something that didn't make any sense to me at all and to not even question it – that is, to work the 12 Steps on *faith*.

Given my long mental health history, the 2nd Step: "Came to believe that a Power greater than ourselves could restore us to sanity," was extremely attractive. I had had twenty-five years of psychotherapy and psychoanalysis with six different psychiatrists, and "all the king's horses and all the king's men couldn't put Humpty-Dumpty together again." Let's face it, I had been a basket case from the get-go, ever since I was four years-old and used to play at the other end of the playground, because I thought all the other kids were against me.

These 12-Steppers were telling me with this 2nd Step that some *Power* (they don't mention *God* right off the bat, because they don't want to scare us away), merely a "Power" I am able to acknowledge as being more powerful than myself (that was easy, in the mental state I was in I perceived everybody around me as more powerful than me) – could be the doorknob, could be the group – that this Power, whatever it is, has the capacity to cure me of my mental illness. The word "restore" didn't apply to me, because I never had been sane in the first place. I knew that.

And then the 3rd Step: "Made a decision to turn our will and our lives over to the care of God *as we understood Him*," told me how to activate this Power from the 2nd Step in my life. All I had to do was to turn myself in, to turn myself over to the Big Warden in the Sky. Well, that was easy! I had been a fugitive all my life. I was ready.

For the next four months I set about going to 12-Step meetings and working the 12 Steps with a vengeance. As sick as I was, I figured I had to work like a beaver in order to catch up with all those "earth people" out there. I worked the first three Steps somewhat, but mainly I concentrated on the 9th Step: "Made direct amends to such people wherever possible, except when to do so would injure them or others," and the 12th Step: "Having had a spiritual awakening as the result of these steps, we tried to carry this message to alcoholics, and to practice these principles in all our affairs."

I wanted to make amends *fast* to all the family members and friends I had hurt, and then to become an A.A. "expert" or maybe a "saint," so I could cure other people. I had a sponsor (someone who helps you to work the 12 Steps) in the very beginning, but I fired him over a political argument. I can do it on my own, I thought.

("Working" the 12 Steps, for those who are not already members of a 12-Step program, means reading about, writing about, thinking about, and/or talking about a certain Step, coming into some sort of agreement with it, and trying to apply it directly to your life with some type of positive action.)

I immediately wrote letters to my two ex-wives, children, and old friends, apologizing for all the trouble I had caused in their lives when I was drinking. I sent money to employers I felt I had cheated. With less than two months of sobriety, I volunteered my services at the local intergroup office, typing volunteer phone lists one day a week.

I took on 12-Step service commitments at the meetings, like making the coffee, putting out the literature, taking care of the group treasury. In search of a paying job working with alcoholics, I moved to another town and became a professional alcoholism counselor. I threw myself body and soul into the 12-Step program and especially the 12th Step (helping others).

In the new town where I moved I got another sponsor and worked one Step a month, until by the end of my first year of sobriety I had worked all 12 Steps as thoroughly as I thought they needed to be worked. That's that, I thought. Now I can "go back out there in the stream of life."

One night, while working the graveyard shift as a facilitator at a local alcoholism treatment facility, it occurred to me that what I *really* needed to do was to try to get back with my second ex-wife (the one I had tried to push out of the moving car going 50 m.p.h.). The logic of it was pure and simple. We had always loved each other before, and now that I was sober and cured of my insanity, wouldn't we really make a great pair? It didn't matter that a year ago she had said she didn't love me and had divorced me. All that would change, I was convinced.

I quit my job at the treatment center, loaded all my stuff into my new used car, said good-bye to my West coast friends, and headed back across the United States to the town where I had left my two ex-wives and the three ex-kids. It seemed at the time to be the perfect solution. The perfect ending to a happy story.

Upon my return to the scene of my past drinking and drugging, everyone was delighted to see me and to see that I had been clean and sober for over a year. However, my second ex-wife didn't want to take me back. I couldn't believe it. The shock of that rejection put me into a suicidal anxiety-depression that lasted for seven months. I didn't think about drinking and using drugs. I was working the 1st and the 12th Steps so thoroughly that I had lost my obsession for alcohol and drugs entirely. I just wanted to die.

Every morning I woke up begging God to take me somehow – I didn't care how – cancer, an auto accident, murder. I didn't have the nerve to kill myself. The anxiety was so bad I felt like I was being immersed in a huge vat of ice water, despite the fact that it was summer and the temperature outside was in the 90's. My chest felt like a gorilla was sitting on it. I couldn't breathe. I didn't have the strength to walk around the block, although up until then I had been running three miles a day.

All this, and I was going to three 12-Step meetings a day, hauling halfway house clients to outside meetings, making coffee, and chairing a 12-Step program committee in an Alano

Club, where I had to recruit sixteen different meeting speakers a week. I was working the 1st the 12th Steps with a vengeance. They call this "two-stepping."

It was then that I met the man who was to become my third sponsor and who was to show me that working the 12 Steps is a *lifelong* proposition, and that *all 12* of the 12 Steps must be worked on a daily basis, if one wants to obtain "quality" sobriety.

We started over with Step 1, and this time I admitted I was powerless not only over alcohol, but also over every other aspect of my life, including whether or not my second ex-wife took me back. I hated being so dependent on my ex-wife that I would want to kill myself, or her, just because she wouldn't have me. I could see it was a sick dependency (the basis of codependency), where I was virtually without my own self-worth, even my own identity, without the "significant other" to live through vicariously. This addiction to the other person was more painful than anything I had ever known with alcohol and drugs.

I learned also, in addition to the powerlessness and surrender so necessary in Step 1, that a strong belief in a Power greater than myself (Step 2) was critical to the working of the rest of the 12 Steps. Unless I had some Power to which to turn, my own powerlessness would be unbearable. This meant I had to take a stronger look at the "God" question, and to start to formulate some hypotheses about that Higher Power. After all, if I was not drinking after twenty-seven years of trying not to drink, *something* with some element of kindness must be helping me now.

Without beating around the bush, up until this time God "as I understood God" was a kind of whimsical Son of a Bitch who arbitrarily dealt out rewards and punishments to us guinea pigs here below, expecting a level of perfect behavior of which none of us was capable. It wasn't that I didn't *believe* in God. I believed in Him plenty!

Sure, in the peaceful moments when my life was going well, I indulged in the academic entertainment that there was no Creator, and that it all just came into existence on its own, but when the going got tough, I would always send up a plea for some help from Somewhere, usually trying to make a little deal to go along with it. God, if you do this, I'll do that.

Now, my back was against the wall once again. For over a year God had given me everything I had wanted: sobriety, good jobs, casual love affairs, enough money to pay off my debts and buy a car, new friends, and the return of old ones. I was floating on a pink cloud of spiritual bliss. God was my Good Buddy. But now, a huge tragedy had fallen on my head. My second ex-wife wouldn't take me back, which meant I was doomed to live out the rest of my life a hopeless old bachelor, unwanted and alone.

Rejection, alienation, and death! It was too much for me to bear. I wanted to die. God was a Bastard now. How could God *do* this to me? How could I practice the 3rd Step and turn my will and my life over to the care of a God who could be so cruel?

My third sponsor insisted I needed to work the 2nd and 3rd Steps without evaluating the results (or God). He wanted me to accept the fact that my second ex-wife didn't want me and to go on from there, without judging the outcome or God. He maintained that God's will would turn out to be the best thing for me. He wanted me to accept this on faith. I wasn't prepared to do this at the time. I just couldn't accept the "unacceptable." Instead, I wallowed around in self-pity, until another casual love affair came along to rescue me, and then I went back out West to continue working professionally with alcoholics.

However, it was during that second year of sobriety that I first began to get an inkling of the profound depth of my addiction to women and to having some female in my daily life who could "fix me." I was actually making these women my *God*. Slowly I began to identify the addiction and to see how it worked in every area of my life. I was slowly reaching a *bottom* on codependence as an addiction and slowly breaking through the denial.

It was also during that second year that my third sponsor got me actively involved in re-working the 4th Step: "Made a searching and fearless moral inventory of ourselves." I had done a cursory 4th Step when I first got sober, and then promptly dismissed the need for further self-searching on the grounds that I didn't want to be too self-centered. Without going into specifics, history is filled with philosophers and theologians who have pointed out the importance of "knowing thyself."

In fact, to know oneself is the basis of modern psychotherapy. To live a full, happy, and productive life, *knowing* yourself (your behaviors, your desires, and your character traits) becomes a lifelong process. And so the 4th and the 10th Steps (the inventory Steps) become extremely useful and necessary tools for living, for normal people as well as for those of us who are addicted to various tangible and intangible people, places, and things.

Working the 4th Step is not only a good way to distract ourselves from obsessing over people, places, and things; it is an excellent way to take charge of our own lives. If we take our eyes off those around us and focus them on ourselves, we find things about ourselves that we can actually change. The area I found in myself which needed the most changing was my *character*, those aspects of my personality which had been causing me trouble for years and to which I now began to realize I was addicted. The tendency to hold onto resentment was one.

If you do something to hurt my feelings, I'll hold onto it

forever like a bulldog with a bone. That's just the way I am, I guess, because that's the way my family of origin was. But knowing where it comes from doesn't release me from the compulsion to harbor resentments. During the three months it took me to do that second 4th Step, I listed eighteen pages of resentments toward people and institutions in my life. Some of those people had been dead for twenty years.

What causes a human being to hang onto displeasure and anger toward a dead person for twenty years? What possible *payoff* could reinforce such an obsession? In my case I discovered I needed that righteous indignation like a drunk needs a drink. It gave me a sense of completion. I wasn't myself unless I had my bag of resentments along with me, and if I forgave the bastards that meant I couldn't be *right* any longer. But let me tell you, the indigestion, anxiety, and sleepless nights that went along with being "right" cost me dearly over the years! Migraine headaches, skin problems, bronchial difficulties. Resentments can eat you alive. They say that a resentment is like taking poison and expecting the other person to die.

Working that second 4th Step, I learned that listing the resentment, the person, the cause, how it affected me, writing out the prayer, and acknowledging my part in it had a cathartic effect on the obsessive-compulsive nature of the resentment. Praying for the other person and myself helped a lot, too. I was able to let go of many of my resentments in my second 5th Step: "Admitted to God, to ourselves, and to another human being the exact nature of our wrongs."

Some of my resentments have proved more addictive than others, and I am still working the 12 Steps on them after all these years, admitting that I am powerless, that my life has become unmanageable, that there is a Power that can take them away, and becoming willing to turn them over to that Power.

During the second year of my sobriety, I found it necessary

to start keeping a journal – a written account, expression, and communication – of my thoughts and feelings over the years. I didn't write in it every day, only when I felt the need to. It acted as an ongoing personal 4th, 5th, and 10th Step. Sometimes I read parts of it aloud over the phone to others.

Sometimes I Xeroxed pages and passed them around. Sharing our experiences with those who suffer from the same addictions is an integral part of the letting go process of becoming free from those addictions. It becomes a lifelong process for one such as myself, whose addictions and maladaptive behaviors range far and wide.

At the end of four years of sobriety, I returned to the city I got sober in and promptly went into another suicidal anxiety-depression, this time because I wasn't able to succeed at the artistic career I had been pursuing. It took me ten months, diligently working the 12 Steps, before I was able to let go of that particular anxiety and depression. All this time the idea of drinking alcohol or using drugs never entered my mind.

I was working several other 12-Step programs and struggling with my many other addictions, but the original 12-Step program I came into seemed to have relieved me of my obsession to drink and use drugs for good, or so I thought.

And then one summer day, while returning from a meditation retreat in the Southwest with seven years of sobriety, I was driving across the high desert happy as a lark, happier than I had ever been in my life, when the idea of taking a drink occurred to me. I started noticing the little red neon signs in the windows of the bars in the little towns I drove through. I thought, since my life is going so well, why not sweeten the pot with a little drinkeepoo? And, then, of course, a few of my favorite drugs would make it even sweeter!

The insidiousness of the diseases of alcoholism and drug addiction is implicit in this incident. Let no man or woman think he or she is ever cured! After over seven years without the slightest thought of drinking or using, my mind came up with the desire to get drunk and stoned, and the craving was so strong that I began to imagine myself actually doing it. First, I thought, I would stop at the next bar I found and have a few beers. Then I would buy a bottle of bourbon and see if I could score some marijuana and a few pills. Then, I would get a gun and proceed to pick up some extra spending money.

As these plans filtered through one part of my brain, another part of my brain was watching them and thinking, how insane can you get? Alcohol and drugs ruined your life for twenty-seven years, and now you want to do it all over again? Thank God, I did not drink.

The same insanity came to me just before my ninth sober birthday, only this time it was even crazier. Part of my story, which I will go into later, is that I originally came into my first 12-Step program because I became obsessed with killing people. My last few drunks in 1979, I would be in a bar, shooting pool, and I would get this crazy idea that I just had to pick someone out in the bar, wait for him outside after closing time, and beat him to death with a two-by-four.

This is not a pretty thing to admit, but it is part of my story, and I believe I have to tell it if I want to avoid doing it someday. Once again (this time with nine years of sobriety), part of my brain was thinking about drinking and killing people, and another part of my brain was able to recognize the insanity of it! Again, I did not drink.

I learned three things from those two experiences with the renewed craving for alcohol and drugs. First, that my addiction for alcohol and drugs is never cured. It is always right there, just below the level of my consciousness, ready to raise its ugly head and bite me again. That is why no matter how long I remain clean and sober, I will always continue to be dependent upon working the 12 Steps on my addiction to alcohol and drugs, for the rest of my life if I wish to remain clean and sober.

Second, that just because I *want* to drink and use doesn't mean that I *have* to. *Wanting* to drink doesn't have to mean *drinking*. Today, even if I want to drink, I can choose *not* to – just for today. And third, that working the 12 Steps is the last (and the best) resort I have for dealing with my addictions, whatever they are. Nothing else but the 12 Steps has, or will, work for me today.

Today my freedom from alcohol and drugs is contingent upon my attendance at 12-Step meetings. Groups that practice the 12 Steps on various *tangible* addictions, such as Alcoholics Anonymous, Cocaine Anonymous, Marijuana Anonymous, and Narcotics Anonymous, are very necessary support systems for those alcoholics and drug addicts like myself, in order to provide a *fellowship* for the practice of the 12 Steps. I have also discovered that the 12 Steps are very helpful in many *other* areas of my life.

Groups that practice the 12 Steps on various *intangible* addictions, such as Al-Anon, Adult Children of Alcoholics, Codependence Anonymous, Emotions Anonymous, Emotional Health Anonymous, and The 12 Steps for Everybody, are very helpful to those of us who suffer from anger, anxiety, depression, and negative thinking.

Let me tell you in the following chapters how the 12 Steps can work on addictions other than alcohol and drugs.

Chapter 2

CIGARETTES

When I went to my first 12-Step meeting in 1979, the person who took me was a member of a church I had been attending for two-and-a-half months. He was also a sober member of that particular 12-Step program and became my first sponsor. A "sponsor" is someone who introduces you to a 12-Step program and helps you to start working the 12 Steps.

We would stand out on the patio together after the regular church service, while the rest of the congregation was getting their juice and cookies, and guiltily smoke our cigarettes over in the corner to one side. Everybody else sort of snobbishly ignored us. I remember wishing I didn't have to continue with that grubby cigarette smoking habit.

I heard a non-smoker once say that smoking a cigarette was like "licking an ashtray." It made me feel embarrassed and disgusted with myself. If the 12 Steps work on alcohol and drugs, I thought, why wouldn't they work on cigarettes, too?

Ever since I was seventeen, alcohol and cigarettes went hand in hand for me like salt and pepper. I would take a swig of beer, and then I would take a drag off my cigarette. I smoked about a pack a day when I wasn't drinking, but I would smoke a whole pack in one evening, if I was drinking.

Cigarettes for me were also a big part of my "macho" image. The literature and the movies of my generation strongly promoted the smoking of cigarettes as a way of proving you were a man. If you had a smoking cigarette dangling out of your mouth that meant you meant business.

It also meant you were sexy. Men and women alike were portrayed as highly sexual and romantic figures if they smoked cigarettes. In fact, what was the first thing you did after you had sex? Have a cigarette, naturally! If you didn't smoke, you were considered to be some kind of church-going "square," a religious fanatic prude who didn't deserve to have fun, or sex, even if you wanted to. How was a person expected to give up cigarettes under those conditions?

Cigarette smoking was also considered a highly acceptable form of relaxation and social activity. If you took a break, naturally you smoked a cigarette, and naturally you offered a cigarette to the person you were with. Two people sitting together, French inhaling and "spit-firing" cigarette smoke from their nostrils, was as natural as Fibber McGee and Molly, as American as Mom's Apple Pie.

You'd be a Weirdo Commie Pervert if you turned down the offer of a cigarette. And besides, what would you do with your hands if you didn't smoke? After all, even condemned criminals were given one last cigarette.

Over the twenty-seven years I drank booze and the twenty-five years I smoked cigarettes, I must have tried to quit a hundred times or more. Every month, it seemed, I was trying some new plan to give up smoking. I would count the number of cigarettes I smoked in a day and make complicated charts and graphs, trying to taper off with the "numbers" game.

I would chew gum or eat candy all day long like a cow. One stop-smoking plan had me taking a drink of water every time I wanted a cigarette. I floated to the bathroom every ten minutes. Another plan suggested a deep breath of fresh air to quell the craving for smoke. I ended up hyperventilated and dizzy half the time.

There were movies about filthy smokers' lungs and lobectomies, horror stories of cancerous deaths, sheet after sheet of tar-stained Kleenex. Nothing worked. I finally made the conscious decision that if I had to die, smoking cigarettes was just as good a way as any to go. Then, aside from my usual chronic colds and shortness of breath, I developed a terrible sore throat.

The pain often felt like someone was driving a pencil through the front of my throat, just about where you would put a tracheotomy tube if you had to place one. I had seen people with those tubes in their throats and heard the way they had to learn to talk, by inhaling and expelling breath over their vocal cords.

I went to the ear, nose, and throat doctor, just praying that I didn't have throat cancer, but also hoping he would tell me I had to quit smoking. I needed some strict authoritarian direction (as if that ever worked on any of my addictions). No, I didn't have cancer, just a sore throat, and no, I didn't have to quit smoking, just cut down. What a laugh! When had I ever been able to "just cut down" on anything?

At the end, my drinking, marijuana smoking, and cigarette smoking were all so intertwined that I couldn't do one without the other. I would quit one and the other two would hook me again. If I quit all three and then "slipped" on one, I would soon be hooked on the other two. It got to be real complicated, as complicated as multiple addictions can be, as they drag us helplessly through life, costing us money, ruining our health, affecting our jobs, and destroying our lives and the lives of those around us. Sound like fun, doesn't it? I used to think so.

So, when I saw that the 12 Steps were working right off the bat on alcohol and marijuana, as well as other drugs, I thought, why not throw the cigarettes in with them and give it all up at once? To make a long story short, it worked. I was able to take Step 1 on cigarettes without equivocation in that I could see I was addicted, that I was powerless over cigarette smoking, and that my life had become unmanageable from that particular addiction.

I had reached a painful bottom, not only with the chronic colds, shortness of breath, and painfully sore throat, but also with the self-esteem problem I was having at the church. I was sick and tired of being sick and tired of being a smoker. I was ready to surrender it, let it go, and turn it over to a Power greater than myself. I had tried everything else and failed. The 12 Steps were the last resort, and they worked.

Let me correct that – they *work*, but they only work *one day at a time*. Because I am not cured of my cigarette smoking addiction, and I never will be. As soon as I think I am cured from any addiction, it is my wholehearted opinion that I am doomed to return – to cigarette smoking, or alcohol, or drugs, or whatever my addiction is. Maybe not today or next week or even next year, but eventually the addiction, no matter what it is, will raise its ugly head again at a time, when not *working* the12 Steps, I am just as powerless as I was before. And then before I know it I will be back in the bag again, "lighting up" one more time.

How many of you have done that? How many of you have tried to give up something, made all kinds of promises, and then just when you thought you had it licked, *whammo*, there you were again, doing what it was that was ruining your life enough to cause you to quit in the first place? Does that fit the definition of insanity – doing something again and again, over and over, that didn't work before?

This means I have to *work* the 12 Steps on a daily basis with respect to cigarettes. If I see someone smoking a cigarette and it looks good to me, I have to remind myself that cigarette smoking is something I am powerless over, and that if I start up again, my life can quickly become unmanageable. I remember that a Power greater than myself can help me not to smoke, and I quickly make the decision to turn my craving for cigarettes over to that Power right away.

I share my experience, strength, and hope with others who are *not* smoking one day at a time, and I am always on the lookout for a newcomer, a likely prospect who seems ready to quit smoking. When I find one, I gradually open up the idea that it is possible to stop, if he or she is really ready to do so. I offer to take them to a 12-Step meeting if they want to go, or to help them work the 12 Steps on smoking, if they want to.

It is not necessary to be pushy. If they are not ready that means they haven't had enough *pain* yet from cigarettes to cause them to do what is necessary to stop. You can't help someone who has not *suffered* enough yet from their addiction and is not ready for help.

A person may think they are ready to give up an addiction, when actually they are not. They might cry or rage that they've tried everything, that they're willing to "go to any lengths," but when it gets down to the bottom line, they aren't. They simply will not go to the meetings and work the steps on a daily basis.

When you run across someone like this, you're wasting your time and energy to pursue the question further. They haven't had enough of whatever it is they're addicted to, and nothing you can do or say is going to change that until they have had *enough*.

I also work Step 6: "Were entirely ready to have God remove all these defects of character," and Step 7: "Humbly asked Him to remove our shortcomings," on cigarette smoking, whenever I think of it. These are the Steps that demonstrate our readiness, willingness, and openness to have God, as we understand God, take an active part in our lives. They go hand in hand with Step 3: "Made a decision to turn our will and our lives over to the care of God *as we understood Him*."

All my life I tried to be the "master of my fate and the captain of my soul," ever since society told me that that's what a "man" is supposed to do. In fact, that poetic phrase was created for me, and *My Way* was my theme song. They told me I could be President of the United States if I wanted it bad enough and tried hard enough, but I couldn't even quit cigarettes. Over and over, "my way" failed. Maybe it doesn't for other people, but it sure did for me. I've got the evidence to prove it.

I've heard some people criticize the 12 Steps for being a "cop-out." They say that turning your will and your life over to God is sheer laziness, an unwillingness to take responsibility for your own life. Nothing could be farther from the truth. Turning my will, my life, and my addiction over to God is creating a partnership with the Creator of the universe, the most powerful Force in the universe; and when I do that it shows that I am willing to become *fully invested* in the responsibility for my own life.

Working Steps 3, 6, and 7, where we make a decision, become entirely ready, and humbly ask for help from Whoever or Whatever we consider God to be, does not mean that we then sit back and do nothing more on our own behalf. Instead, we take an *active part* in letting go of our addictions by continuing with the spiritual processes of surrender, faith, self-discovery, forgiveness, self-disclosure, acceptance, amends, meditation, and working with others.

We do not abrogate our responsibility for our own lives; we form a true partnership with God, as we understand God. This is what working the 12 Steps is all about. It's not only a medicine, a psychology, a theology, and a philosophy – it's a fully *comprehensive* way of life. And we do it on a daily basis.

Attendance at Smokers Anonymous or 12 Steps for Everybody meetings is an integral part of the practice of the 12 Steps on smoking for some people. At the meetings you find the loving support and the experience, strength, and hope to *not* take that first cigarette, cigar, or pipe, one day at a time.

Naturally I am not going to be able to work every one of the 12 Steps on every addiction every day of my life. I wouldn't have time to breathe if I did. What I mean by working the 12 Steps on a daily basis is that I am always ready and willing to work the 12 Steps on *any* of my addictions at *any* time, and when the opportunity presents itself, I jump at it.

In addition, as I make my way throughout the day, if something doesn't seem to be going right in my life, I try to come up with a Step that will be at least part, if not all, of the solution. Working one or more of the 12 Steps on a daily basis is a spiritual way of handling addictions that cannot be handled in any other way if you are an addict like me, and for me cigarette smoking is one of those addictions.

Chapter 3

ANGER

In the "Introduction" of this book I talked about trying to push my second ex-wife out of a moving car going 50 m.p.h., and in Chapter 1, I briefly mentioned my murderous rage in that last bar shooting pool, which initially brought me into my first 12-Step program.

How is it possible for anyone to become addicted to anger? Don't we usually think of addictions as having some *tangible* goal like alcohol, drugs, food, money, or people? We know that *anger* is an emotion, a feeling. How can one become addicted to a feeling?

From my earliest days I suffered from temper tantrums, fits of anger so intense that I can assure you many others suffered from them, too. I often cried myself to sleep with frustrated fury over the fact that my parents wouldn't come into my room for one more "good night."

When my baby sitter didn't give me what I wanted, I stamped on her feet with my shoes. She was too old and too slow to get out of the way. At the age of four I split my baby brother's scalp open with the wing of a toy metal airplane, and at age five I chased a neighborhood friend down the street with a spade, because he wouldn't play in my sandbox the right way. He defended himself by throwing a bucket at me. I still have the scar on my upper lip to prove it.

I won't go into the long list of my childhood rages and battles. I could write a whole book about my inability to handle the emotion of anger. The funny thing is I was usually such a quiet, well-behaved guy. I could go for days and even weeks without feeling or showing any anger at all. And then I would explode like a bomb and everybody around me would get hit by the fragments. It was just like my drinking. I was a "periodic" when it came to alcohol and a periodic when it came to anger, too.

My father and mother were the same way. My dad, who drank periodically, was almost always angry, especially between drunks. We would wait for him at night to come home from work, wondering if he was going to be drunk (which would make my mother angry), or if he was going to be angry (which would fill us all with fear and trembling). Our house was like a mausoleum, it was so permeated with tension and uncertainty.

When my father was angry he would explode and get violent at the drop of a hat. If you spilled a crumb at the table, you were taken back and laid across the bed for a whipping with Dad's leather slipper.

I became so sensitive to my father's moods out of fear of being beaten, or of losing his love, that I would question him constantly as to how he was feeling, whether or not he was angry. Sometimes I would question him so relentlessly that, even though he wasn't angry to begin with, he would *get* angry, which brings us to the strange phenomenon of "mixed addictions."

In the incident of the ex-wife and the moving car, I was angry with her because I thought she had snuck off with another man for the forty-five minutes I was in the psychiatrist's office. (She'd have to be pretty fast on her feet, wouldn't she?)

Two addictions, and probably more, were in operation here. The primary addiction was codependence, that insane and absolute dependence I had on the *woman* for my self-esteem and well-being. The secondary addiction was anger. I needed my anger fix that morning, because I felt like such an insignificant little "snit" coming out of the psychiatrist's office, and any excuse to be angry, no matter how farfetched, would serve to start my anger binge. It gave me a sense of "self."

Despite the fact that it had only been a forty-five-minute psychoanalytic session, when I came out of the elevator and didn't see my wife sitting in the waiting area, I naturally assumed (my self-esteem being lower than a worm's) that she had taken that opportunity to be with another man. Isn't that what most women would do, while waiting for their husbands in the psychiatrist's office?

Armed with righteous indignation at my wife being with another man (my suspicion made it fact, because it so happens I am addicted to paranoia, too), I was then free to work myself into a rage becoming "drunk" with anger, so filled with fury that I attempted to murder her on the way home by trying to push her out of the moving car.

Closely related to the phenomenon of mixed addictions, such as the codependence and anger described above, I also discovered another peculiar phenomenon, which I call the "two-sided coin" behavior of addictions.

It seems that just as I was addicted to my own fits of anger as a young child, I also became addicted to my father's rage. Strange as it sounds, and even though I dreaded my father's anger more than anything and told myself that I didn't want him to be angry, I really did. That's why I kept asking him if he was angry, testing him to see if he was ready to explode. My *fear* was actually my *desire*. Sigmund Freud was right.

Sometimes my brother and I would even do things on purpose just to make my father angry. We were addicted to the adrenalin, the excitement, and the drama that was generated by my father's anger; and we were willing to pay the price of a spanking to get the fix of our father's anger, the same way that a drunk is willing to pay the price of a hangover.

This bizarre phenomenon, the two-sided coin aspect of some addictions, is both intriguing and elusive. It is difficult enough to break through the denial system of an addiction such as anger, but to be addicted to *acting out anger* as well as being addicted to *having someone angry at you* is so unbelievable, so contradictory in theoretical terms, that the denial system of such two-sided coin addictions is often safe from discovery for a lifetime.

My mother's anger on the other hand was different from my father's. She did a long, slow burn, which lasted for weeks, months, even years. My mother once said she had grown up in a household so filled with shouting and other expressions of anger that she had made herself a promise she would never get angry when she raised her own family. Quite a promise, huh? A human being who never gets angry! Once she got so angry she spanked me with the "spiked" end of a high-heeled shoe.

But that was rare. Usually my mother's anger showed itself as *silence*. The silent rage of the martyr. I felt my mother's anger, it seemed, almost all the time. She was either angry or "depressed" (another addiction that is often mixed with anger). And with these two role models, my father and my mother, I became addicted to those two types of anger, the explosion and the silent burn.

I probably would have been the same if I had been raised by Eskimos. Whether or not it was modeling or genes or hormones or what, where my addictions come from is of absolutely no use to me, when it comes to getting rid of them. And it is certain to me now that anger is definitely one of my addictions.

When I was married, I was usually angry at my wife and kids for some reason or other, anything at all, really. If I didn't have a reason I often made one up. I left my first two wives because I felt they didn't appreciate me enough. Who *could* appreciate someone who was always angry?

When I had a job, I was usually angry at my boss and my fellow employees. Either they weren't behaving the way I thought they should, or they weren't treating me the way I thought they should. Over the years I have had about fifty jobs I quit because I didn't think I was being treated fairly enough.

I would get drunk or stoned or overeat, just to try to cope with the anger. Nothing worked. I would sober up, clean up, lose weight, and then in a few days I would be angry all over again. I needed that anger like a gambler needs a bet, like a drinker needs a drink, like an overeater needs an apple fritter.

To repeat a question we asked ourselves earlier, don't we usually think of addictions as having some *tangible* goal like alcohol, drugs, food, money, or people? Isn't that what "fixing" is all about? We get that funny feeling in the gut, that *hole* that cries out to be filled, and we reach out and grab whatever stuff is around to fill it. We satiate ourselves and the "hole" feeling goes away, only to return some few hours later, like the proverbial aftermath of a Chinese dinner.

But, it also happens there are *other* addictive things that will fill that hole, and you don't have to be able to *touch* them for them to work. These are the *intangible* addictions such as anxiety, depression, guilt, paranoia, and obsession. These are *feelings* and *ideations* rather than objects; however, we can still use them to excess just as we can use *objects* to excess. Anger, too, is one of these intangible addictions.

Everybody gets angry. It's only human. In fact, it's not healthy to repress anger or any other emotion; and there are all kinds of therapies developed to get us to feel our feelings and to express them. The difference between *healthy* anger and *addictive* anger is the same as it is between healthy drinking, eating, or shopping and addictive drinking, eating, or shopping. The difference is *excess*, and you can measure the level of excess by the level of *negative consequences*.

You can tell the difference in the results. The healthy behavior is *constructive* and brings a sense of well-being; the addictive behavior is *destructive* and brings a sense of misery – to ourselves and to others in the family and the community at large. That's what addictive anger does. It destroys your health, your job, your relationships, and the community around you.

Every addiction has a *payoff*, a goal or combination of goals that will conspire for a time to fill that hole the addict cannot tolerate. What is the payoff for addictive anger? Several things.

First of all, when you get angry you get lots of attention. People tend to listen to an angry person. There is something hypnotic about angry people. And you get both positive and negative attention – positive attention when your anger causes others to do what you want them to do, and negative attention when others move away from you out of fear or retaliatory anger.

You might also even get into a good fight, which is a more intense form of attention. Whatever the results of your anger, you are sure to get a reaction one way or the other, and getting reactions from people is another form of addiction.

Secondly, anger gives you power and control. You notice that many people will give in and give you what you want when you get angry. Anger then becomes a tool for manipulating the world around you to your own advantage.

A third payoff an anger binge is certain to bring is an adrenalin rush. Adrenalin is that hormone your body puts out when it needs to be hyperactivated. The synthetic is epinephrine, the drug they give patients on the operating table to raise blood pressure and stop bleeding. Adrenalin is a kind of "speed," and God knows I never turned down a jolt like that when it was offered to me before I got clean and sober. The body can become addicted to adrenalin rushes, and anger is a good way to give yourself a "belt."

Another payoff from anger is the drama and mental excitement it creates in our lives. Those of us who were raised in alcoholic or dysfunctional families grew up sensitized to seeking drama and excitement the same way you might crave tuning into the same TV soap opera every day, just to see what kind of insanity is going on in the lives of the characters on the screen.

Excitement is a fix for boredom, that uncomfortable feeling we all get when we're alone with ourselves for too long and don't have anything to keep us entertained. And so rather than having to face that painful emotion of boredom, we get angry and generate excitement in order to mask the boredom and make our lives interesting.

Anger gives us a feeling of righteousness and justification. After all, we have a "right" to be angry at whatever it is that's making us angry, don't we? Otherwise, we wouldn't be angry! Being *right*, we can also feel superior, a feeling highly prized among those of us who usually suffer from extremely low self-esteem.

Is there any doubt that we would want to seek situations where we can indulge in anger, when we know we are going to get attention, a reaction, power, control, a rush, drama, excitement, justification, and superiority? Anger situations for the anger addict are like bars for the alcoholic, or gambling casinos for the compulsive gambler. We find these situations impossible to resist.

Anger gives us a reason to live, a problem to solve, and a neurological fix. I believe the nervous systems of addicts are quite different from those of the average human being. We addicts are wired differently, that's all. Either the neurons are too large, or the dendrites are too long. The synapses are too far apart, or the neurotransmitters are too strong or not strong enough. You figure it out.

All I know is that I'm wired differently than normal people, and that anger (as well as fear, guilt, joy, and just about any other strong emotion you can name) is an experience that my body not only does not handle very well, it also *craves*. That is the main phenomenon of addiction. *That which we do not handle well, we also crave*. Knowing all of this now, what do we do about it?

When I came to my first 12-Step meeting, I was not in touch with my anger. I *felt* my anger but I was not "in touch" with it. There's a difference. You see, when you give up one addiction like alcohol, drugs, food, or people, other addictions like anger, fear, depression, or paranoia become more intense. And sometimes they come flooding in quite quickly.

I was three months sober and sitting in a 12-Step clubhouse, waiting for the 12-Step meeting to start and looking around at the people there, when suddenly I realized that I hated everyone in the room, and I wished I had a submachine gun so that I could mow them all down. Just another little homicidal fantasy, nothing serious. But this time it was different. This time I *realized* I was angry, that I had this hostility, this intense rage toward these fellow suffering human beings, and I *realized* I had had this anger for a very long time.

I was getting *in touch* with the anger. I was getting awareness, insight, *self-realization*. And then I realized that it didn't make any sense! It wasn't rational. Why should I feel angry at those people? They didn't do anything to me. In fact, they were there just like I was, trying to stay sober and trying to help others to stay sober. They were good people, not bad people.

And I realized that this feeling of hostility I carried around with me was really very uncomfortable. I was getting sick and tired of the anger and the uncomfortable feeling it brought with it. I hated that feeling of anger. I resolved right then and there that I wasn't going to feel angry at the people in the 12-Step meetings anymore, that I was going to try to let go of the anger. I was starting to reach my bottom on anger.

So that we do not confuse "normal" anger with "addictive," or excessive, anger, let's reiterate what was said in an earlier paragraph. Everybody gets angry. It's only human. In fact, it's unhealthy to repress anger and there are many therapies designed to open us up to the feeling of anger and the beneficial expression of it. The difference between *healthy* anger and *addictive* anger is that healthy anger is constructive and brings a sense of well-being, while addictive anger is destructive and brings a sense of misery to ourselves and to those around us.

It was two years after that clubhouse meeting, where I first got in touch with my anger, that I finally *really* reached my bottom on addictive anger, while working in a public detox for skid row alcoholics.

It was my job in the detox to get the drunks undressed, showered, gowned, fed, and in bed upon their arrival. Sometimes a certain amount of physical force was necessary to manage this task. I knew I was still practicing addictive anger, despite the fact that I had been working the 12 steps on it occasionally. I had even prayed to God that God remove my anger, because I found myself from time to time using what I considered to be *unnecessary* force on the skid row drunks. They made me angry, and so I felt they "deserved" it.

In their drunkenness the detox patients were often verbally abusive and insulting. Sometimes they even became physically violent and combative, and then we had to defend ourselves and put them into restraints. The job gave me a good excuse to get angry and to get physically violent with my anger. But every time I did, I felt bad about it, knowing I could have really handled the situation more peacefully if I had wanted to.

One night I was in the shower room with a known violent drunk, alone, and he was mouthing off at me and being his usual abusive self. I had had rough dealings with this man before. I felt the anger rise in me like those cartoon characters that turn red from the feet up. I could have gone for help, but instead I tried to manage him by myself, and when he finally attacked me with a chair, I threw an arm lock on him and broke his arm. I heard it break. I still feel bad about it to this day.

They never found out at work that it was me who broke that drunk's arm. Everybody just naturally assumed he had broken it out on the street before he came to the detox, but I knew. And I felt sick about it for weeks. That was my bottom on anger. I got sick and tired of being sick and tired of getting out of control with anger. From then on I have tried to work the 12 Steps on anger in earnest at every opportunity.

Some people wonder why we 12-Step people keep telling these gruesome stories about the wreckage of our past. Is it because we want to impress people or to wallow in self-pity or guilt? Is it because we get some kind of perverse pleasure out of the unmanageability of our lives before we gave up the addictions? Maybe so, maybe not.

In my case, I believe it is necessary to remember where I came from, so that I will not have to return there. To keep my addiction to anger in complete remission, I must work the 1st Step on it for the rest of my life, admitting my powerlessness over anger and reminding myself how unmanageable my life can become if I allow myself to indulge in addictive anger again.

I do not believe I can get away with working the 1st Step *just once* on anger, or any other addiction I might have. I have already discovered that when I ignore the 1st Step on excessive anger, it slowly starts to come back, and it is not long before I start turning red from the feet up all over again, over some situation in my life that I can usually handle quite peacefully, once I decide to act sanely. God will step in, if I ask for God's help.

As often as I can remember it, I come to believe that a Power greater than myself can restore me to sanity and take away my addictive anger (Step 2). On a regular basis I make the decision to turn my will, my life, and my anger over to the care of God, as I understand God (Step 3).

Continually taking the 4th, 5th, and 10th Steps on anger, I tell that story about breaking the drunk's arm whenever the occasion arises, along with other equally humiliating stories about some of the irrational things I used to do in a state of anger. I also promptly admit I am wrong, any time I let my anger get out of control enough that it causes damage to myself and to others. Openly sharing my experience with my anger might someday help someone else to identify their own addiction to anger, thereby bringing them closer to their own bottom (Step 12).

Isn't it interesting that it took *two years* from the time I decided I wanted to give up anger in that clubhouse meeting, to the time in that detox shower room that I reached my bottom on anger and was *truly ready* to work the 12 Steps on it? As they say in the 12-Step programs, "it takes what it takes." Another saying is "time takes time."

In order for me to become entirely ready to have God remove all these defects of character (Step 6), including anger, I usually have to become so pitifully and incomprehensibly *demoralized* by my behavior that I am willing to go to *any lengths* to give it up. And any lengths for me means working the 12 Steps (all of them) on a continual basis on each and every one of my addictions (defects of character).

Humility – humbly asking God to remove our shortcomings (Step 7) – is a key word for me. I used to try to let go of these destructive behaviors on my own, and it never really works for very long. Without God's help I just don't seem to be able to do it, and God's help doesn't seem to come unless I have reached a sufficient state of humility (lack of pride). Reaching a state of humility for me usually means being humiliated over and over again by the same character defects/addictions, until I am down on my knees and ready to ask for God's help.

Getting *entirely* ready to humbly ask for God's help on any addiction is a critical prerequisite to letting go of that addiction. Some 12-Stepper once said: "If ya' just kinda wanna give up drinkin', ya' just kinda keep on drinkin'." The same holds true for any addiction. Some kind of "bottom" has been entirely necessary for every addiction I've ever really confronted. Which brings me to what I believe is the only valid working definition of addiction. *An addiction is any behavior that YOU are willing to go to any lengths to give up.*

As you can see, the key word is "you." No one else can say whether or not your behavior is addictive. No doctor, lawyer, or Indian chief can pronounce you addicted to anything. *You* are the world-renowned authority on yourself. Only *you* know when you're sick and tired of being sick and tired of whatever maladaptive, irrational, or addictive behavior you have.

Only you can do anything about it. You are the only person who can take the necessary steps to help yourself. And only you can work the 12 Steps that will liberate you from your addiction. No one else can work them for you.

As for the 8th and 9th Steps on anger: "Made a list of all persons we had harmed, and became willing to make amends to them all," and "Made direct amends to such people wherever possible, except when to do so would injure them or others," if I went around apologizing to everyone in my life who I ever hurt with my anger, it would be a full-time job.

What I did was write letters and speak to the main sufferers of my anger, conveying my apologies as best I could for the things I used to do when I flew off the handle. Some of them responded positively; some did not. I felt better knowing I did what I could by making the effort to apologize.

But I believe the best amends I can make today is by "living well" and setting a good example. I believe instead of apologizing for the past, that we need to focus on living *non-addic-*

tively in the *present*. Right living and right action are the keys. This means not stifling our anger, but rather expressing it in rational and moderate ways. Moderation, the avoidance of excesses or extremes, is a way of life that brings peace and love, rather than pain and strife.

Before I ran across the 12 Steps, I never did anything in moderation. Maybe that's why I consider myself the "World's Most Addicted Person." It's okay to have feelings. Nobody's saying it's not. But *my* emotional system is used to the *all-or-nothing* principle when it comes to feelings, and that's what has been getting me into trouble all these years.

The amends Steps (8 and 9) and the 10th Step ("Continued to take personal inventory and when we were wrong promptly admitted it.") are designed to encourage us toward moderation in *all* our affairs. I work Step 10 continually, taking my mental and emotional pulse on my level of anger as often as possible, and promptly admitting I am *wrong* when my anger level becomes excessive or destructive.

True moderation was not possible for me, until I started practicing the 11th Step: "Sought through prayer and meditation to improve our conscious contact with God *as we understood Him*, praying only for knowledge of God's will for us and the power to carry that out," on a daily basis. Without prayer, and especially without meditation, I would not be able for very long to let go of addictive anger – that explosive rage over which I used to smash objects.

It took me two-and-a-half years of sobriety to reach my bottom on anger, and it took me another two-and-a-half years to get to the place where I was willing to meditate on a daily basis. Daily meditation is what keeps my emotional balance intact. It calms my nervous system so that things don't get out of control. It is the conscious "plugging in" to that Power greater than myself, so that I can experience the serenity and joy that is life without addictive anger.

Finally, Step 12: "Having had a spiritual awakening as the result of these steps, we tried to carry this message to alcoholics, and to practice these principles in all our affairs" is applied by substituting the words "anger addicts" for the word "alcoholics." In other words, we anger junkies take the opportunity wherever we find it to tell our stories to anyone we think might have a problem with anger, too. This doesn't mean you go around the streets collaring everybody you see in a rage and trying to convince them to work the 12 Steps on their anger. You could definitely expect your hospital bills to rise dramatically if you did this.

What I do is wait until I hear somebody saying that *they* think they have a problem with anger before I say anything to them. If they're starting to recognize this addictive defect in their character, then I start talking about how I have the same problem. And if they're interested in hearing more, I tell them what I do about it. You can't carry the message to anyone who is not yet ready to hear it; and they are not ready to hear it until *they* say they are without my prompting. This is only my personal opinion.

"Practicing these principles in all our affairs" means acknowledging and performing in our daily lives the principles of powerlessness and surrender, letting go and letting God, self-discovery and self-disclosure, forgiveness and acceptance, amends and restitution, meditation and prayer, and working with others, also know as love and service.

Is this an impossible task? Many have found it so, and they continue to suffer from their various addictions. Others find that it is possible to make the effort, and that simply making the effort brings not only untold relief from our addictions but also tremendous spiritual rewards. Serenity, peace of mind, joy, bliss, and love are some of the payoffs from merely attempting to practice these principles in all our affairs.

Love and service, in order to overcome the addiction to

anger, begins with attendance at 12-Step meetings like Emotions Anonymous, Emotional Health Anonymous, and The 12 Steps for Everybody. These 12-Step groups address many of the intangible addictions – the addictions to mental and emotional excesses.

At these 12-Step meetings we listen to the stories of others and decide for ourselves whether or not we belong, whether we qualify for a 12-Step program or not. Going to these 12-Step meetings and communicating our experience with others, who suffer from the same intense mental and emotional distress that comes from practicing habitual anger, is a very necessary part of maintaining our freedom from the addiction to anger.

Is it really worth it? Is it really worth the trouble to follow the 12-Step path? The answer for me is a resounding "yes!" My only alternative to practicing the 12 Steps on my various addictions is the pain and suffering that comes when I practice the addictions themselves. Today, by working the 12 Steps, it is possible for me to choose the less painful way, the way of happiness, joy, and freedom.

Chapter 4

FOOD

When I was a kid, there was nothing I enjoyed more than eating a whole one-pound box of chocolate-covered cherries at a single sitting. I was in seventh heaven when chocolate-covered cherries were dribbling out of my mouth. There were forty to a box, and I would count them one-by-one as I ate them, only wishing that somehow they would last longer than I knew they would.

My brother on the other hand would always save his, savoring them over a two-or- three-day period, but I would finish mine off in a couple of hours. There was no way I could save mine. Once I ate *one* chocolate-covered cherry, I was hooked until I had eaten the whole box. It was that *one* that set off the phenomenon of *craving*. After that I was a goner. Then I would try to figure out some way to con my brother out of some of his.

But when I was a kid there was never any question about me having a weight problem. I was as skinny as a rail. I could metabolize an elephant, if I could get one in my mouth. My basketball coach in high school called me "Horse" because I ate like one. I could eat anything and not gain weight. And, so, I didn't think I had a problem with food.

In my 20's and 30's, alcohol, drugs, and cigarettes took the place of food. I was always drinking a beer, smoking a cigarette, or "toking" on a joint. Sometimes I was doing all three at the same time. I had to have something going into my mouth in order to try to fill that gaping hole, that insatiable "cave" inside us addicts that never really *ever* gets filled; no matter how much we take into it.

Of course, whenever I smoked marijuana I would get the munchies, and then I would have to go to the pancake restaurant and have a Spanish omelet with pecan pancakes topped with boysenberry syrup. And then, naturally, on the way home I would have to stop off at the donut shop and pick up a half-dozen apple fritters. And apple fritters wouldn't be anything without a pint of fudge ripple ice cream to go along with them now, would it? I think you get the idea. *And yet for my age and height, I was not overweight*.

It was not until I had been clean from booze, drugs, and cigarettes for about two years that I began to take a look at the possibility that I might be a compulsive overeater. I was working the swing shift in a detox where all the nurses brought in food dishes, and we had a smorgasbord going all evening long.

"Have some of this!" "You've got to try some of that!" they'd say, and for me it was awfully hard to turn down a request from a woman in uniform. One bite led to another and before long I was thirty-five pounds overweight. I had become a human garbage can. I would eat anything anyone shoved in front of me, and anything you left on your plate, too.

One morning I couldn't get out of bed. I had to roll off onto the floor, get up on my hands and knees, and then stand up like a baby. I could have used a crane to get up. It was then I knew that I had reached my bottom on food, and that I had to start working the 12 Steps on eating.

I admitted I was powerless over food and that my life had become unmanageable. I came to believe that a Power greater than myself could restore me to sanity in the area of food and could take away my desire to overeat. And I made a decision to turn my will, my life, and my food-problem over to the care of God, as I understood God.

Unlike alcohol, drugs, and cigarettes, which are possible to give up entirely, food is not possible to abstain from completely. *You have to eat food in order to live*. I made up my mind I was going to eat three moderate meals a day and nothing in between. I also made up my mind I was going to try to abstain from sugar. Almost everything has sugar in it, even ketchup, so I decided to be *specific.*

I told myself I would eat no more "cookies, candy, cake, or pie," and anything else with sugar in it I would try to keep to a minimum. I had a specific weight goal in mind – 175 pounds. I also had a specific weight loss goal in mind – two pounds per week for seventeen-and-a-half weeks, totaling thirty pounds. I kept tabs on myself with a bathroom scale every morning and night.

Using the 12 Steps on compulsive overeating, I lost the thirty-five pounds in one month! Whenever I had the desire to eat and it was not mealtime, I worked the first three Steps automatically in my mind. ("I am powerless over food; my life has become unmanageable. I believe there is a Power that can help me. I turn my craving for food over to that Power.") I did the same thing whenever I had the desire to eat more than a moderate meal. Sometimes I would recite the first three Steps on food to myself a hundred times a day.

I also went to 12-Step meetings that deal with compulsive overeating, in order to work Steps 4 through 12. I shared my food story with other compulsive overeaters, took an inventory of myself with respect to overeating, and admitted to God, to myself, and to other human beings the exact nature of my wrongs in the area of overeating.

It is very important to work the 12 Steps on a daily basis, because only by going to 12-Step meetings and working the 12 Steps on a daily basis does the addiction to food, or anything else, lose its power over us. The meetings and the 12 Steps *generate* a connection with a Higher Power, which enables us to *overcome* the power of the addiction. We *get* the power from a Higher/Greater Power. It's a paradox. By admitting we *don't* have the power, we *get* the power from God.

And it is a *temporary* gift, on loan to us as long as we continue to work the 12 Steps on a daily basis. The meetings provide a place for us to work the 12 Steps in their entirety. The meetings are a place where we are *reminded* to work the 12 Steps. They are a place where we come into contact with others who are working the 12 Steps, and thereby we stay in contact with a Higher Power of our *own* understanding.

At the daily meetings I was able to practice self-discovery, self-disclosure, and forgiveness, which are integral to Steps 4, 5, 8, and 10. I was able to practice acceptance, readiness, and humility, which are integral to Steps 6 and 7. And I was able to practice making amends, which is integral to Steps 9 and 12.

Nowhere is it easier or more convenient to work with others than at a 12-Step meeting. Making amends for the wrongs we have done others in the past and helping others today by sharing our experience, strength, and hope in recovery are the two most important actions I can think of in all of the 12-Step programs.

If I don't try every day to *help* other human beings with the same problem that I have to *help themselves*, then I get the feeling I'm "dying on the vine." In the 12-Step programs they say, "You can't keep it unless you give it away." A great Spiritual Leader once said faith, hope, and charity were the Big Three in leading a spiritual way of life, and the greatest of these is charity, which we interpret as Love.

When we put the power of Love to work in our daily lives by practicing the 12 Steps and working with others, our addictions shrivel up and go into remission. When we ignore the power of Love in our lives, those addictions flourish and dominate our lives.

Over the past twenty-six years my craving for food and my addiction to compulsive overeating has returned many times. This tells me that I am never cured, only in *remission* on a daily basis. I can tell when it's happening, because I start obsessing over food. I start looking forward to meals, sometimes days in advance. While I'm eating breakfast, I'm thinking about what I'm going to have for lunch. I hardly even taste the food while I'm eating it. I'm just desperately trying to fill that gaping hole in my soul with as much food *or whatever* as possible, as fast as possible.

When this happens, I know I'm practicing my addiction again. In the words of another 12-Step program, I have only "a daily reprieve, contingent upon the maintenance of my spiritual condition."

Just recently I went on a three-week vacation and gained eight pounds, overeating. I had not been to a 12-Step meeting on compulsive overeating for over a year. I knew what I was doing, and I went ahead and did it anyway. I knew I was going to have to pay the price. It took me over a month of "starving" to lose the eight pounds, plus the feelings of guilt and shame that went along with losing control again – one more time. The 12 Steps are always there for us to use, but even so, we don't always use them.

A word to those of us who are addicted to more than one substance, thought, emotion, or behavior. When I speak of going to daily meetings, I do not mean that it is possible to attend every 12-Step program that I qualify for on every day of the week. There aren't enough hours in the day for that. Whatever the addiction or program, whether it involves the *tangible* addictions, such as alcohol, drugs, nicotine, food, sex, or gambling, or the *intangible* addictions, such as anger, personal relationships, anxiety, depression, or negative thinking, a 12-Step meeting is a 12-Step meeting.

A 12-Step meeting is a place to work the 12 Steps on the addictive behavior that will destroy my life, if I do not work the 12 Steps on it. I try to go to at least one 12-Step meeting a day, whatever the addiction or behavior, because I believe that my life depends on it. I know that my happiness depends on it.

Adversity in the form of physical, mental, emotional, and spiritual discomfort motivates me to go to the 12-Step meetings on a daily basis. If I miss a day or two, I start to feel "squirrelly" in some area of my life. When I go to the meetings I feel better. I believe adversity and the pain it brings with it are a must for character growth, and character growth is a must for spiritual growth. Spiritual growth is where it's at for me today.

Attending 12 Step programs that deal with compulsive overeating or eating disorders, such as Overeaters Anonymous and The 12 Steps for Everybody, can be a very helpful support in letting go of these types of tangible food addictions.

The positive results and great rewards I have experienced in twenty-seven years of working the 12 Steps on various addictions have not been so much in the areas of money, property, or prestige as they have been in the areas of love, joy, and serenity.

The dropping away of anxiety, depression, anger, guilt, shame, and paranoia have been the results of working the 12 Steps. A feeling of warmth and compassion toward others, a sense that all is well with the world, an exhilaration at the sights and sounds of the universe around me, and a peace of mind and quiet contentment that nothing before has ever brought – these are the rewards of going to the 12-Step meetings and working the 12 Steps on *whatever*.

Chapter 5

FAMILY MEMBERS

Family members who live with an alcoholic, drug addict, or neurotic often become just as sick as the alcoholic, drug addict, or neurotic with whom they are living. These constitute "dysfunctional" families, and every member of the family is probably going to suffer *some* destructive aspects to their own character and behavior, which will adversely affect their life and the lives of those around them. That is, until their own destructive character flaws (addictive behaviors) are successfully addressed.

Seventy years ago I was born into an alcoholic, dysfunctional family, and I have been living with the addictive effects ever since. My father was an alcoholic and my mother was the daughter of an alcoholic. I consider myself lucky that they didn't start abusing me, until I was around two years-old.

My father loved me and my mother hated me. Then they would switch roles; my mother would love me and my father would hate me. They took turns playing nice cop, mean cop, and I never knew who was going to be which. I got real good at being the victim, the villain, and the volunteer. Even today sometimes when I nurture myself I feel guilty about it and have to do something to punish myself. It is very difficult in my own mind to conceive of the notion that I deserve anything good in my life.

In those early childhood years I became addicted to ambivalent, vacillating personalities, dramatic situations, violent excitement, and guilt. I learned how to be a chronic doormat and a people-pleaser. I also learned how to be a controlling, manipulative tyrant who would do anything to get my own way.

Power in interpersonal relationships became a critical factor in my survival. I thought if I couldn't control a situation I was going to be victimized by it. It was that old two-sided coin behavior again. Either be on top and get what I wanted or else be a doormat and a victim and give everybody else what they wanted. There was no in between or moderate range for me.

Most of the relatives on my mother's side of the family were children of alcoholics; and most of the relatives on my father's side of the family were alcoholics. When we got together for family reunions it was like the Vietnam War. My mother served Agent Orange for breakfast. My grandfather was an alcoholic. My father was an alcoholic. All of my uncles were alcoholics. There were so many alcoholics in our family, one liquor store sent us all a free Christmas turkey every year.

My father was usually drunk when he stood up at the head of the table to carve the bird. Inevitably he would hit the turkey in the wrong place with a knife or fork, and it would go skidding off the table into my grandmother's lap. Then my Uncle "Bo" would take out his false teeth and put them in my mother's hand when she wasn't looking. Uncle "Jeff" would crack a raw egg on top of his bald head and let it run down over his face. My father would go into a rage and fall into the Christmas tree. All the lights in the house would short out, and it would take an hour to find a fuse.

Doesn't it sound exciting? It was! That's how I became addicted to excitement and drama. And as the years rolled by, a remarkable thing happened. I found myself choosing friends who were either children of alcoholics or alcoholics themselves. I became addicted to relationships with damaged people just like me, and we played "damaged-people" games like "Kick Me!" "Who's the Boss?" and "Let's Do It My Way."

We also played "Fix Me" or "Fix You," whichever happened to be up on the menu at the time. In these damaged relationships there was always a lot of "helping" going on. Let me help you...to do it *my* way! I was quick to perceive what was wrong with you and naturally my brilliant, educated mind had the solution to all of your problems – let's do it my way!

If you didn't do it my way I was very good at being a martyr. Then I would *sacrifice* my way. We would do it *your* way, and I would suffer. I was very good at suffering, because I had such low self-esteem that I could generate a lot of sympathy, pity, and self-pity out of sacrificing my way for yours. Either way, I had you.

People-pleasing, problem-solving, over-achieving, enabling, suffering, judging, controlling, criticizing – these are the addictions generated by the family disease, the "family member addictions," which come from being raised with, or living with, alcoholics, drug addicts, neurotics, and other dysfunctional people. We become dysfunctional people ourselves, if we were not already born that way.

I don't know whether it's genetics, environment, or glands that play the causative role in the addictive behavior of the family member. I suspect it's all three. But once again, it's not *where* it comes from that counts in recovery; it's what we're going to *do* about it that counts, that has any meaning or significance. And the only thing I've found that works on these family member addictions is working the 12 Steps on them on a daily basis.

What are the *payoffs* for the various aspects of the family disease? Let's take problem-solving, for example. Problem-solving keeps our *minds* active and busy so we don't have to *feel*. We family members will choose *thinking* over *feeling* any day, because feeling means experiencing shame, guilt, fear, and rage. We will do anything to avoid these painful feelings. So we put our minds to work solving problems, usually other people's problems, although we also spend a lot of time obsessing over our own.

When we solve a problem we experience momentary self-esteem, something we are sorely in need of, since our self-esteem has usually been running on empty for years. If we can solve the boss's problem, the spouse's problem, the kid's problem, or the friend's problem, we might even get some *approval* (love, of course, would be too much to ask for). Just throw us a little approval. It's like bread crumbs to a starving person.

Coming up with the solution to the problem actually entitles us to run the show, doesn't it? It's a sanction to manage, an authorization of power, to have the *answer* to the problem. It's also a form of people-pleasing and over-achieving. There are many types of payoffs to the addiction of problem-solving. And the same is true of enabling, suffering, judging, controlling, and criticizing. The question now is, how do we gain freedom from suffering these family member addictions? The answer is simply by working the 12 Steps.

Twenty-five years ago I attended my first 12-Step program for family members, because I couldn't get my patients sober in the detox where I worked. I couldn't even get my own daughter clean and sober from alcohol and drugs, despite all of my knowledge and experience in the field of alcoholism and drug addiction treatment. How humiliating that was and how helpless I felt. What a blow it was to my ego! My ego doesn't like being disappointed; it's very sensitive that way. So I came into the 12-Step program for family members to learn how to get *other* people sober, and there I learned how to work the 12 Steps on my *own* family disease. It was definitely not an easy task at first.

The whole concept of my *not being responsible* for the well-being of others simply flew past me like a jet plane. After all, wasn't it my *professional* job to get people sober? And when I was a kid, wasn't it my *job* to please my parents and to do what they wanted? And when I married my first wife and had two children of my own, wasn't it my *job* to love, care for, and protect them all, as well as to manage, direct, and control their whole lives?

What was love anyway but complete commitment and total responsibility for the person you loved, the *other* person? Great religious leaders had taught me: "It is better to give than to receive." Putting other people first and myself last had become a way of life for me! In fact, it had become an addiction in its own right.

In the 12-Step program for family members, I learned that I had everything completely backwards. I learned that the only person I am responsible for today is *myself*, and that everyone else is responsible for themselves, whether they like it or not. I learned that I am *not* responsible for another person's well-being or happiness, and whenever I think I am, tremendous resentments build up, not only in me but in them, too.

Is it any wonder that my wives and children became angry and frustrated under the weight of my overbearing caretaking? Is it any wonder that I became furious and exhausted with the thankless task of running their lives? In the symbiotic relationships I had created with family and friends, the family disease ran rampant, and the knowledge of this alone was not sufficient to put *me* into recovery.

In order to begin *my* recovery from the family disease it was necessary for me to work the 12 Steps on each of my family member addictions. I had to admit I was powerless over the lives of others – that my life had become unmanageable. I had done everything I possibly could to get my daughter to stop drinking and using, and everything I had done had failed. I had to admit I was powerless over her addictions, and that my life had become unmanageable.

I had to come to believe that a Power greater than myself could restore us to sanity – my daughter and myself. Neither of us had the power to get her clean and sober and neither of us had the power to get me off her back. It was necessary for me to come to believe that some Power (God, the Great Spirit, the Universe) could do for us what we could not do for ourselves.

This 2nd Step does not say that we believe that Power *will* restore us to sanity; it says we believe that Power *could* restore us to sanity. There's a big difference. This Step acknowledges that God *can* do it. I believe we come later to find through experience that He, She, or It *will* do it...in time. But, it is not up to *us* to determine *when* it should be done, or how long it should, or will, take. I have spent a lot of my life agonizing over the "unrestored sanity" in this world.

And, so, I have to be very careful not to speculate about when, how, or in what area God will restore me to sanity. If I lay expectations on the Higher Power, I am *playing* God. Believing in God is the basis of faith. Believing God is all-good and all-powerful paves the way for a confident faith and trust. Trying to figure out what God *should*, or *will*, do or *when* God will do it is *playing* God, and playing God can get me into all kinds of trouble. The foundation of the 2nd and 3rd Steps for me is to have *faith* in my Higher Power, rather than trying to *understand* my Higher Power.

The 3rd Step was very important for me when I learned that cocaine dealers were calling my fifteen year-old daughter's house and threatening to cut off her legs, because she wouldn't pay them the money she owed them. At the time I desperately had to make the decision to turn my will, my life, and my daughter's health and safety over to the care of God, as I did *not* understand God. (My third sponsor often said: "If I had a God I could understand, I wouldn't want Him.") I had to have faith that God would do the right thing by my daughter, whatever God's will for her was.

Along with the 2nd Step, the 3rd Step puts the final touch on our commitment to a complete faith and trust that some all-powerful and benevolent Power in the universe will take care of things the way they are supposed to be taken care of, given the fact that we've done everything we possibly can up to this point. When I learned my daughter's life was in danger due to her drug-dealing, my natural tendency, given the realization that calling the police would be about as useful as wheels on a sailboat, was to go buy a gun and go after the cocaine dealers myself. Without the 12-Step program I might even have done that.

But thanks to having worked the 12 Steps for over two years at that time, I knew taking the law into my own hands was not the answer. At least I could see God had restored me to *that* much sanity. I had already talked to my daughter until I was blue in the face, trying to get her to give up her lifestyle.

No, by the time they were ready to chop off my daughter's legs, I was ready to work the 12 Steps on my daughter's situation, in fact, on my daughter's entire life; and I believe this readiness, driven by pain and desperation, was what enabled me to take the 3rd Step so completely with respect to my daughter's well-being and my responsibility for it. Today, twenty-six years later, I am happy to report that my daughter still has her legs. God did for us what we could not do for ourselves.

After taking the first three Steps, which I consider to be mental and philosophical adjustments, working the last nine Steps is the *concrete action* necessary to complete recovery in every area of our lives.

Some might consider our admission of powerlessness and the surrender of our will and our lives to a Higher Power to be a passive way out. Whether or not this is true, Steps 4 through 12 are definitely the aggressive and energetic actions we need to practice for the rest of our lives, if we expect the Higher Power to do His or Her part in it. As my fourth sponsor, an alcoholic priest, once said: "It's like riding a bicycle; I pedal and God steers."

In the case of giving up my addiction to running my daughter's life, the pedaling I did was to work the remaining nine Steps. I had to do a 4th Step and make a searching and fearless moral inventory of my behavior over the years with respect to my daughter. I had to do the 5th Step and admit to God, to myself, and to another human being the exact nature of my wrongs in my daughter's case. This included admitting I was not responsible for her well-being, and I was wrong to think I was.

I had to do the 6th Step and become entirely ready to have God remove all my defects of character, including the misapprehension that I was responsible for running my daughter's or anybody else's life. And I had to do the 7th Step and humbly ask God to remove my shortcomings and to take away my desire to protect and control my daughter.

Some people might exclaim: "How horrible! How can you say you don't want to protect your own daughter? It's unnatural for a parent not to protect his or her own child."

Wrong! What's unnatural, even *insane*, is the intense obsession I carried over the years to obsessively and compulsively look after every one in my life that I love. Although this delusion is readily understandable, considering how we were trained, we soon come to realize that it's just another *addiction*, picked up in our childhood from others who suffered the same addiction, and born in an over-protective atmosphere of fear and paranoia.

Naturally, I love my daughter and want her to live a happy and healthy life. Naturally, I want to protect her from anything and everything. But the worse thing you can do to another human being is to take away his or her right to live their own life, and that includes learning how to protect themselves. Animals know this and they force their young out of the nest at an early age.

But, we humans hold onto our children for as long as we can; in fact, we often seem bent on working out our own neurotic fears and obsessions on them; they, the very ones to whom we should be giving the most freedom to make their own mistakes and to grow in their own way.

If I made a list of every time I advised, told, or controlled my children for their own good, it would be as long as this book. I always thought I had only their best interests at heart. I have come to realize most of the time it was actually my own fear, guilt, or paranoia that drove me to obsess over and compulsively manipulate their lives. No one is to blame. I am *addicted* to this behavior. But, now that I know this, I *am* to blame if I don't *do* something about it, something to free myself from this horrible obsession.

Let's take the case of my daughter and the cocaine dealers. As it turned out, the Higher Power intervened and my daughter kept her legs. Perhaps she even learned something from the experience about not ripping off cocaine dealers. Maybe she even decided not to use cocaine any more, unless she could afford it, or to learn how to make money in some less dangerous way. If I had intervened, we wouldn't know the answers to these questions because she wouldn't have learned any lessons at all. She might even have stolen from them again and that time they might have really cut off her legs.

The point is, I finally allowed her to be responsible for her own actions and it worked. And even more important, I went ahead and lived my own life. Because the only crime greater than living another person's life is the crime we perpetrate against *ourselves* by taking the time and attention away from our *own lives*. We cannot truly love or be of real benefit to others, until we can first learn to love and be of benefit to *ourselves*.

Continuing with working the 12 Steps on my addiction to run my daughter's life, I worked Step 8 by becoming willing to make amends to my daughter for the years I interfered in her life. With Step 9, I made direct amends to my daughter, apologizing for my meddling and assuring her I was going to try to "get off her back" and to let her live her own life.

Aside from that one direct apology, most of my amends to my daughter have been an attempt to relate to her in a new way, a way marked by courtesy, respect, and compassion, as one human being to another, rather than as a parent to a child. Her response to this treatment is quite positive after all those years of tyranny. She even calls me sometimes to ask for feedback on some situation in her life. I try to share my own experience without giving advice to her. I am making what is called "living" amends.

The last three Steps, 10, 11, and 12, are the "Maintenance Steps" which enable us to live reasonably, sanely, and relatively well among and with people today.

Step 10, continuing to take personal inventory on my behavior toward my daughter and promptly admitting when I am wrong, is necessary on an ongoing basis. I work Step 11 on my daughter by seeking through prayer and meditation to improve my conscious contact with God as I understand God, praying only for knowledge of God's will for me in the area of my daughter and the power to carry that out.

Without this consistent communication with my Higher Power, my own addictive ideas quickly return to get me into trouble. I sometimes even get the crazy idea I know what's best for my daughter. Can you imagine how fast this throws a monkey wrench into what has become a peaceful and loving relationship between us?

Step 12 with respect to my daughter means continually carrying my experience, strength, and hope to others who suffer this same addiction – the addiction to assuming responsibility for, and control over, the lives of our loved ones. Whenever I come across someone who seems ready to surrender this addiction, I share my 12-Step message with them. I don't dump it on them or even foist it on them. I simply speak of my own experience in this area and if they identify, fine. If not, that's fine too.

It is no longer my job to change other people or to run their lives. And this is the way I practice these principles in all my affairs, because just as I have come to realize I cannot be responsible for or control my daughter's life, I know now I cannot do this for anyone else. And you would be surprised how much this has improved my interpersonal relationships with everyone around me.

One piece of 12-Step literature says that unless we are painstaking in our efforts, the results are nil. According to the dictionary, "nil" means "nothing." Some people give the 12 Steps a superficial run-through and then wonder why the Steps are not working very well in their lives. Still others may get a few results and think there's nothing to it; then when the "crash" of anger, fear, despair, guilt, shame, or paranoia comes, they look around and wonder what happened.

I've already had the opportunity to see what happens when I let up on my 12-Step spiritual practice. I immediately experience the return of "stinking thinking." This includes the desire to drink and use, the desire to overeat, feelings of intense rage, and the desire to run other people's lives, just to name a few. The point here is that if I want to remain entirely *free* from the family member addictions, I have to continue to work the 12 Steps on all of them on a continuous basis.

A bottom composed of physical, mental, emotional, and spiritual pain motivates me to work the 12 Steps on a continuous basis. It provides a readiness and a willingness to practice the principles of the 12 Steps daily in all my affairs. However, I didn't reach a bottom on all of the family member addictions at the same time.

Problem-solving, over-achieving, enabling, suffering, judging, controlling, criticizing, obsessing, negative thinking, ambivalence, vacillation, drama, excitement, control, power, damaged people, being a martyr, self-pity – each of these addictive elements in my family disease "module" came to a head in its own time and in its own way.

And, as each of these addictive defects of character surfaced, it became necessary for me to work the 12 Steps on each. I had to admit I was powerless over my compulsion to over-achieve and that my life had become unmanageable. I came to believe a Power greater than myself could restore me to sanity and take away my compulsion to enable the damaged people around me. I made a decision to turn my will, my life, and my suffering over to the care of God, as I understood God. I made a searching and fearless moral inventory of myself in the area of judging others.

I admitted to God, to myself, and to another human being the exact nature of my wrongs when it comes to criticizing people, places, and things. I became entirely ready to have God remove my negative thinking, and I humbly asked God to remove my addiction to ambivalence.

I made a list of all the people I had been vacillating with and became willing to make amends to them all. I made direct amends to those people I had sought out in my life simply because they were dramatic and exciting. I continued to take personal inventory on my tendency to be a martyr, and I sought through prayer and meditation for God's guidance as to what I should do about my self-pity.

I tried to carry my experience, strength, and hope in all these areas to those I believed were ready to hear it and ready to let go of their own family member addictions.

During my early years in the 12-Step programs, while I learned about my family disease and the family member addictions that go along with it, I also discovered I had a special set of addictive character defects, which seemed to be connected to being the adult child of an alcoholic. These were low self-esteem, people-pleasing, "doormatism," shame, guilt, fear, rage, self-destructiveness, feelings of not belonging (alienation), stuffing feelings, and co-dependency. I was blind to these particular addictive aspects of my character, until I went to my first 12-Step meeting for the adult children of alcoholics.

I sat behind a man who shared that his mother had sexually abused him as a child. Later that day I realized with horror that the same thing had happened to me, and I had blocked it out all those years. That revelation was so painful I didn't go back to that meeting for another three years. And when I did go back I was to discover still more disturbing things about myself and my relationship with my mother.

I learned I had a tendency to be a doormat and a people-pleaser. I would do almost anything to get people to like me, and in the process I often let them walk all over me. I was great at *giving*, but I didn't know how to *receive*. I took whatever salary the boss wanted to pay me and worked whatever hours he wanted me to work. I didn't have the self-esteem to stand up for myself and often had to run away just to protect myself from abusive situations.

I also learned I tended to reject people I liked and to get involved with people I didn't like. The women I picked for relationships were often abusive, and often I tended to abuse them.

I felt guilty about everything. If you sneezed, I felt guilty. My anxiety was always turned up to HIGH, and rage was just around the corner. If I wasn't hitting my thumb with a hammer, I was doing something even more self-destructive like gambling away an inheritance or quitting the best job I ever had, just because they didn't give me enough attention.

When I walked into a roomful of people, it was them against me. Underneath I seethed with violent emotions, but on the surface I was afraid to even blink an eye.

Working the 12 Steps on each of these addictions and

going to 12-Step meetings, I have found that I don't have to be a doormat or a people-pleaser any longer. Other 12-Steppers have shown me I don't have to pick abusive friends and loved ones anymore. I was told that I could learn to love myself and to become my own non-abusive parent, and that is exactly what has happened. What a relief!

I was able to let go of guilt and shame, and I learned how to turn over my fear and rage to God. I was taught how to surrender "pulling the rug out from under myself" in interpersonal, occupational, and financial situations. I came to experience a feeling of *love*, rather than *alienation*, for my fellow human beings, and I became able to risk exposing my emotions to the world around me. Today I feel happy, joyous, and free in these areas of my life, and I owe it all to working the 12 Steps and going to the 12-Step meetings.

Attending 12 Step programs that deal with family member addictions, such as Al-Anon, Adult Children of Alcoholics, Codependents Anonymous, and The 12 Steps for Everybody can be a very helpful support in letting go of these types of intangible addictions.

There are no more practicing alcoholics in my life today. All that toxic drama and excitement is gone. Once in a while someone asks: "Doesn't it get lonely? Doesn't it get boring?" Not really.

Today I surround myself with sober people in the 12-Step fellowships, and I go to lots of 12-Step meetings. In the 12-Step meetings I find real love and constructive excitement. Letting go of the family disease, my life is a safer, saner experience, and the beauty and joy of simple things are much more apparent to me today.

Chapter 6

COFFEE

Is it actually worth the trouble to recognize *coffee* as an addiction and to give it up? I mean, really, aren't we carrying this addiction business too far? What are we supposed to do, become saints? Only you can answer this question for yourself. All I know is what happened to me, and what happened to me was enough of a bottom to start me working the 12 Steps on coffee.

As a child my father used to give me what he called "coffee kunkels," when I asked for them. A "coffee kunkel" was half a spoonful of sugar and the rest filled up with coffee from my father's cup of coffee. Mainly I was interested in the sugar, but I liked the coffee taste too, and I was fascinated by the way my father would sit back in his chair at the end of each meal and leisurely smoke his cigarette and drink his cup of coffee. It seemed to me to be the epitome of serenity and bliss. At that time I began to draw the connection between cigarettes and coffee and *relaxing*.

As for actually drinking coffee myself, I didn't get into that until I was about fifteen. Then I would have an occasional cup of coffee with my father at a restaurant or with my friends late at night, when we were trying to sober up before going home. Coffee didn't become a daily habit for me until I was seventeen and became a daily cigarette smoker.

From the very beginning coffee did a strange thing for me. While others claimed coffee stimulated them and got them going in the morning, my experience was that it always calmed me down and put me to sleep. If I had trouble getting to sleep at night, I would drink a cup of coffee. It also relaxed me to the point where I began to use it as a laxative whenever I was constipated.

Later, when my daughter was diagnosed as hyperactive and given "uppers" to calm her down, I learned that for some of us the chemistry of drugs works differently than for others. Coffee, of course, is loaded with caffeine, which is an alkaloid stimulant. Another interesting alkaloid stimulant is cocaine, although it is classified as an alkaloid narcotic (anesthetic). Some people use this anesthetic drug to "pep" themselves up.

In any event, in the beginning I saw no harm in drinking a few cups of coffee a day with my meals. Like most of my addictions, in the beginning I saw them as beneficial rather than harmful.

In the Army over in Korea I developed prostate trouble among other things, and the doctor said I had to give up coffee as part of the treatment. It was no trouble. I didn't even miss it. When the prostate cleared up I just went back to coffee again. Coffee, like alcohol, drugs, and cigarettes, had become part of that "macho" image I was trying to cultivate, and I saw absolutely no reason to give it up. If I had to suffer that *acid* stomach from time to time that comes from drinking too much coffee, hey, that was just part of the dues of being a man!

And, of course, when I came into my first 12-Step program and started frequenting all those smoke-filled rooms with all those Styrofoam coffee cups floating around, that simply showed me that these 12-Step people weren't goody-goodies, they were real "he-man" type people like I wanted to be. After all, since I had already given up cigarettes, holding a cup of coffee gave me something to do with my hands. I had to have *something* to do with my hands, or else I would melt down into a puddle around my shoes.

I remembered all the "macho" things I had tried to do with my hands when I was trying to give up cigarettes, like flipping a quarter or rolling a fifty-cent piece between my fingers or squeezing a rubber ball to build up my forearms, but somehow the idea of going back to all of that "mishagosh" in place of coffee seemed inappropriate in *real* sobriety.

Instead I just went on merrily drinking my coffee. I mean, really, wasn't the very basis of good fellowship and congenial social activity to have at least *something* to feed down into our body tubes together? Instead of grazing in the pasture or foraging in the bushes, what we did was drink our coffee and nibble our donuts together. If I gave up coffee, I might as well give up people, buy a gun, and shoot myself. What other alternative was there?

And yet, strange things were happening with my coffee drinking. Aside from the recurrent prostate trouble and the acid stomach and the need to urinate every fifteen minutes and the knot in my gut that felt like a wadded dishrag and the periodic headaches, I noticed I was actually getting wired from the stuff they squeeze from those beans that grow on tropical plants in Turkey and Colombia. *Coffee was making me high.*

I noticed it especially in the morning before I had a chance to get food into my stomach. The coffee I was drinking was making my blood race and my nerves tingle. My mind would start going a mile-a-minute, and I would get crazy thoughts and flashback images from bits and pieces of scenes I had seen and been in years ago.

No longer was the drug acting as a sedative and helping me to relax. Now it had turned on me like so many of my other addictions and was starting to take its toll. It was altering my mental and emotional state in ways that seemed detrimental to my well-being.

I wasn't sure whether I wanted this or not. It was like a cheap little "drunk" without losing my sobriety date. And yet I didn't really *like* that feeling any longer. It wasn't really *fun* any more. It was interfering with my serenity and peace of mind. It was distorting reality and reality, no matter how painful it could be at times, was starting to become a valuable and cherished experience for me.

Of course, the coffee high wasn't happening to me *all* the time, only sometimes in the mornings or late at night after I'd had maybe fifteen or twenty cups during the day. Note that my intake had increased sizably from a mere "two or three cups" per day with meals.

I was now working in a place where everybody bought me a cup of coffee every thirty minutes. Then after the evening 12-Step meetings, I would go out with my friends and have a big piece of chocolate cake with chocolate ice cream and a triple espresso coffee with whipped cream to go along with it. "Anything worth doing is worth doing well," my father used to say.

And, yet the prostate trouble and frequent urination and colitis and migraines persisted with a vengeance; and, so I just kind of decided to "kind of" give up coffee. I thought I would just cut down to a few cups a day. And when that didn't work I switched to decaf. Decaf has about one-third the normal amount of caffeine in it, although at the time I was under the false impression that decaf was entirely free of caffeine.

No wonder my "decaf experiment" didn't work either; and within a month I was back to drinking the real stuff and in the same massive quantities as before. I was never really able to quit anything by "cutting down." If you just *kind of* want to give up drinking coffee, you just *kind of* keep on drinking coffee.

And then one day I was sitting in an early morning 12-Step meeting with no food in my stomach and about a half-a-cup of black "go-go juice" swishing around down in there, when I started to feel this tremendous *anxiety* building up in me. My heart started palpitating, my pulse started racing, and I felt that adrenalin jolt of *fear* that sweeps through you during a free-floating anxiety attack.

I also started to *hallucinate*. I heard those little voices I used to hear calling my name when I was drinking and I saw the flashback images, and I began to think about what a good idea it would be to go out and buy a gun and start shooting people. This time I knew it was time, that I had really reached my "bottom" on coffee. I became sick and tired of being sick and tired of getting high on coffee. I shoved the remaining half a cup away from me and said to myself, "No more!"

I decided to quit all forms of coffee, not only regular and decaf, but also coffee candy, coffee ice cream, anything having even the *taste* of coffee. "If you don't want to slip, don't go around slippery places," they say in the 12-Step programs, and I didn't *ever* want to go back to drinking coffee again.

I knew I couldn't avoid people who drank coffee, because that would mean staying away from the 12-Step meetings, and I knew that would be suicide for me. So I continued to go to daily meetings and simply did not drink coffee with the rest of them. Instead, I drank tea (I soon had to give that up, too), or sometimes just plain hot water.

The wonders of plain hot water (the Chinese call it "crystal tea") became intriguing to me. It gives you a nice full feeling without any drugs or calories and keeps a warm glow going down inside your stomach. I drink it today in order to keep my weight down.

But my main line of defense against coffee-drinking was not plain hot water. It was the same program of liberation I use against all of my other addictions – the 12 Steps. I admitted I was powerless over coffee and my life had become unmanageable. I came to believe a Power greater than myself could restore me to sanity and take away my desire to drink coffee. I made a decision to turn my will, my life, and my coffee-drinking over to the care of God, as I understand God. And so forth and so on, right down to sharing my experience, strength, and hope with others who think they have a problem with coffee.

For five years I went without a single taste of coffee of any kind. It seemed I had lost my desire for coffee entirely, until about twenty years ago when I was on a trip to New Orleans and Miami, and my *mind* started working on me again.

What is New Orleans, I thought, without the Cafe du Monde and chicory coffee with beignets (sugar pastries)? And what is Miami without Cuban *cortaditos* (strong espresso coffee with hot milk)?

For the first time in my sobriety, which had included total abstinence from alcohol, drugs, cigarettes, and coffee, and moderation regarding anger, food, and the family disease, I was *planning* a "slip." I was planning to *try* some "controlled" coffee-drinking.

All my training and experience in my *primary* 12-Step program told me that what I was about to do was a terrible mistake. From my observations of others who had tried controlled drinking and drug use, one or two cups of Cajun or Cuban coffee would surely lead me back into twenty cups a day and the insanity of that morning with the free-floating anxiety and the homicidal hallucinations. Was it worth it? Was it worth the risk?

All I can say is that over the last twenty years, sometimes the "coffee-drinking experiment" has worked and sometimes it has not. That first time in New Orleans, I drank one cup of coffee, and in Miami I drank eight cups over a two-month period. Back home for about five years, I was able to control and enjoy an *occasional* cup of coffee. Every time I drank a cup, I felt a slight buzz in my body and my mind started to get a little crazy. I didn't like the feeling, but on the other hand I didn't entirely *dislike* it either. I guess you might say I was using the 12 Steps then to practice *moderation* when it came to coffee-drinking, and I was willing to pay the price of the uncomfortable physical, mental, and emotional feelings that went along with it.

Then, for a period of about ten years my coffee-drinking went out of control again, and I was drinking about forty ounces of strong coffee every day and using it to wash down two large chocolate bars a day. I was getting "high" off the coffee and chocolate, but it didn't seem to threaten my abstinence regarding my other addictions. Finally, I had to give up coffee again, this time for a two-year period. Then, on again for two years. Then, about a year ago, off again. I had reached another physical, mental, and emotional bottom.

I know I am a coffee addict, and I know I am not "cured." I know that the old "insanity" could easily return, if I let my once-a-day coffee-drinking get out of control. What I had done with the "coffee-drinking experiment" was to *try* to move my coffee-drinking from the category of those addictions for which I practice *total* abstinence (alcohol, drugs, cigarettes) into the category of those addictions for which I practice *moderation* (anger, food, the family disease). Working the 12 Steps seems to allow me to do this from time to time, but inevitably I go out of control with coffee and have to return to total abstinence.

Regardless of my behavior, I would *not* risk the catastrophic results of trying "controlled" alcohol drinking, drug-using, or cigarette-smoking. These are addictions for which I *know* I need to practice *total* abstinence all of the time, and I hope and pray my mind never tricks me into thinking otherwise. I don't ever again want to pay the negative consequences for taking even *one* drink, drug, or cigarette.

There is the disturbing notion that some people might try my controlled coffee-drinking experiment with the more dangerous addictive substances – alcohol, drugs, and cigarettes. I've never heard of even *one* case where this has been successful. Such experiments in controlled drinking, using, or smoking inevitably result in the old insanity or death.

Many are never able to return to total abstinence once they get the idea they can exercise "moderation." Playing with the addictions to alcohol, drugs, and cigarettes is like playing with nitroglycerin, or playing Russian roulette with a loaded revolver. I hope I have made it clear how dangerous I believe it is to take *any* addiction lightly.

Today, once again off of coffee, I have found new ways of dealing with my hands at social gatherings and no longer need a glass or a Styrofoam cup to hold onto. The quality of my sleep has improved, and my resistance to colds is better. The stomach pains and migraines are gone. I feel a sense of calm I never knew I had. And what's best of all, that crazy buzz, that insane high that used to come over me when I had too much coffee, has not been a part of my life for over a year.

Once again, working the 12 Steps and attending 12 Steps for Everybody meetings have helped me to do what I could not do for myself, and for that I am truly very grateful.

Chapter 7

CODEPENDENCE

Codependence is a family disease, but because it plays such a strong role in our society today I believe it deserves its own chapter. The beginning of my story on codependence lies in my childhood relationship with my mother, the daughter of an alcoholic father who abandoned her when she was twelve years-old.

All three of the women I married are the daughters of alcoholics who abandoned them when they were young. My addiction to codependence may or may not be founded on my relationship with my mother and mother-substitutes. There may or may not be genetic or hormonal dispositions toward codependence in me as well. The one thing I can be sure of is that the successful "therapy" for my codependence has been the same as for all of my other addictions – the 12 Steps. *Nothing else* has been able to free me from my need to "reunite with the mother."

My mother was a very beautiful and chronically depressed woman. She grew up in a house without any heat, running water, plumbing, or electricity and was forced to go to work full-time on a potato farm when she was fourteen years-old to help support her four brothers and sisters.

Moving to the city when she was eighteen, she went to night school and was hired as a bookkeeper in the large corporation where my father ultimately became president and chairman of the board. My mother and father were a "storybook" couple, until she developed cancer at the age of forty. The disease killed her when she was fifty-two. She died forty-four years ago but my relationship with her is not over yet. I am still getting in touch with the full dimensions of my obsession with my mother.

I didn't become aware of my obsession with my mother until I came into the 12-Step program that deals with the adult children of alcoholics over twenty-five years ago. It's taken me that long to realize that this codependent dynamic between my mother and me actually surpasses addiction and lies in the realm of "faulty ego-formation."

I remained "bonded" with my mother, as I grew up into adulthood, and developed what is called in psychiatric terms, narcissistic-borderline personality disorder. I have found, however, that my tendency to act out of a conglomerate of "false selves" and my codependence on other people, places, and things can be treated as an "addiction" and that it responds quite well to working the 12 Steps on it.

Up until the age of two I was coddled and pampered intensely by my mother. Then when my baby brother came along, I was taken out of the nursery in the master suite at one end of the house and put upstairs at the other end of the house in a small room, entirely alone. At the age of two years-old, I was "exiled to Siberia."

Not only was I abandoned physically; I was abandoned mentally and emotionally by my mother. All of her attention and love now went to my baby brother. My moments with her dwindled to the times when she sexually abused me with an enema tube or beat me with a high-heeled shoe. Experiments with baby monkeys that are taken away from their mothers show them going slowly insane and developing attachments to pieces of wire formed in the shape of "mothers," with buttons for eyes.

Until I came into the 12-Step program that deals with adult children of alcoholics, I had blocked out all of this childhood abuse. When I entered the mental institution at the age of seventeen, under the delusion that my mother was putting poison in the sugar bowl and trying to murder me, the psychiatrist tried to get me in touch with my feelings toward my mother. I went home on a weekend pass and asked her if she had given me much love and attention as a child. She said, "Not after you were two years-old. I felt that little boys didn't really want hugging and kissing after they were two."

Even today whenever someone hugs me, I get a shrinking feeling as though I'm about to be beaten. But it's not as bad as it used to be, and I know that I am slowly getting better, one day at a time.

Growing up, I was quite fearful of girls my own age, until I reached sixteen and started going steady with a girl in my high school class. Until then my codependent relationships had centered around my school and neighborhood male friends. I tended to develop close attachments to friends with whom I would lose my own identity. I was easily controlled and manipulated by them into playing whatever games they wanted to play, going wherever they wanted to go, and doing whatever they wanted to do.

When I got my first car at sixteen years of age, I had so many friends I used to make two trips back and forth between their houses and school in the morning and in the afternoon, just to give them all rides to and from home. I was deathly afraid of incurring their anger or disapproval or of losing even *one* of them.

I desperately needed all of these friends in order to sustain my own *identity*, because when I was alone I felt like a nonentity, no identity at all. That was a very painful feeling. Being alone for me meant overwhelming feelings of anxiety, depression, guilt, shame, paranoia, and low self-esteem. But, by this time I had been drinking alcoholically for over a year. I even had my own phony ID card I could use on the weekends to buy booze at the local liquor stores for all of my friends. I was a very popular guy and had no idea I was risking jail just to practice my codependency and alcoholism.

I was perplexed by my ambivalent feelings toward my

steady girlfriend. On the one hand I needed to be with her; on the other hand I felt intensely smothered and oppressed by her presence and wanted to be alone. After school, necking in the back seat of my car, I would almost swoon with passion and physical fulfillment wrapped in her arms and covered by her wet French kisses, while another part of me felt imprisoned and repulsed, and I wanted to lash out at her and shove her away.

Our loving companionship was often marred by my moody and violent tantrums. I was particularly furious over the way she led me on sexually and then stopped me at the last minute. She seemed to get a kind of sadistic pleasure out of my frustration, or so I thought, and it reminded me of my mother. This was my paranoia.

My relationship with my girlfriend disintegrated into a fit of sullen estrangement. I began to perceive her as my "enemy" rather than my friend. (Later, after working the 12 Steps on codependence, I have come to realize that it has been my own *mind* that has been my enemy, rather than my friend.)

For six years I went without a steady girlfriend, dating sporadically and depending mainly on prostitutes for my sexual activity with women. I was afraid of women. I realized this and almost always had an alcoholic glow on, whenever I went out on a date or had sex with a woman. I needed the false courage of alcohol to anesthetize my feelings of rage, fear, guilt, paranoia, ambivalence, and alienation towards women.

In my early twenties I became a womanizer. This is where the two-sided coin aspect of codependence enters. We are attracted and addicted to those who abuse us, and then we become attracted and addicted to abusing them. The victim becomes the victimizer. The doormat becomes the boot.

I had affairs with several married women and always managed to be going out with two or three single women at the same time. I loved, or was in love with, no one. I was in it strictly for the sex I told myself at the time. Later, I came to realize I was actually in it for the *companionship*, *emotional support*, and *adoration*. My ego/identity needed the attention of these women in order to survive. I was still a "baby," when it came to relationships with women, and men, too, for that matter.

My desperate addiction to women who fulfilled the mother role has never been more thoroughly exemplified than by my marriage to my first wife, the daughter of an alcoholic. I won't go into the nightmare of that marriage other than to say that the basis of our misery lay in the fact that neither of us was able to live up to the expectations of the other. I could not be the father she needed, and she could not be the mother I needed.

I wanted her love and she couldn't give enough. She wanted my love and I couldn't give enough. I wanted her to fix me and she couldn't. She wanted me to fix her and I couldn't. Our desires and our abilities were totally out of line. We were both addicted to abandonment, rejection, insecurity, competitiveness, adversarial confrontations, distrust, resentment, anger, and low or *no* self-esteem.

A horrible thing happens between two people who don't fulfill each other's addictive needs. Anything that remotely resembles love slowly turns into intense hatred, and soon the two unfulfilled codependent people are doing everything in their power to destroy each other.

I reached my bottom on that first codependent marriage, when I woke up one morning and realized I would rather be dead than to stay in that house one more day. I was willing to suffer *any* consequence to escape. Of course, the consequences are predictable for codependents who lose their codependent fixes. We simply want to curl up and die. When I left my first wife, I sank into a deep suicidal anxiety depression that I wouldn't have been able to survive without alcohol and drugs.

While I was withdrawing from that first codependent marriage, I discovered the wonders of better things for better living through marijuana, and I was immediately introduced to another daughter of an alcoholic who became my second wife. We were married only ten days after the divorce became final on my first marriage. We codependents don't like to go too long on our own.

Thus proceeded another eight-year marital hitch inside the bizarre world of codependency, only this time the cannabis drug opened up a new dimension, a form of transference in which my second wife not only played the substitute mother, she also became a means of acting out my many strange sexual fantasies.

A cornucopia of addictions flourished, not only alcohol, drugs, cigarettes, coffee, food, and all of the family addictions, but also pride, lust, envy, greed, anxiety, depression, and guilt.

Whenever a life situation, a person, place, or thing, becomes the focus of such a huge and complex set of addictions, the combined mass of negative energy is capable of developing a monolithic addictive obsession. This is what happened with me regarding my second wife. *I became totally dependent and totally obsessed with her*.

Of all the intangible addictions, the *payoff* for codependence is the most insidious because it is the most primitive and basic to our survival. The payoff for codependence is the care and feeding of the ego, the self, our very corporeal identity.

Without the "significant other," we codependents have *no* self-esteem, *no* identity. We are “zeros,” wandering helplessly and hopelessly in a world of positive numbers. Is it any wonder we are so often willing to suffer anything, *any* pain, *any* humiliation, in order to remain attached to the object of our codependence?

Three times I left my second wife, ostensibly because she

wasn't living up to my expectations, but really because I couldn't bear the pain of the crippling codependence I had on her. When I was a year sober in my first 12-Step program, I traveled thirty-five hundred miles to try to get back with my second ex-wife, and she wouldn't have me. I went into a suicidal anxiety depression that was to become the worst pain I have ever suffered in my entire life.

During that period I was often unable to move, I was so paralyzed with anxiety and depression. I would lie on the floor in my apartment, crying and shaking. Every night I begged God to let me die and in the morning I cursed God for letting me live. This particular "bottom" on my codependence turned out to be the greatest blessing my Higher Power has ever allowed me, because through this pain I had to learn to live without a human significant other, and thus to make *God* my Significant Other.

It took me five years, living alone for the first time in my life, working the 12 Steps in the various pertinent 12-Step programs, to be able to let go of the idea that another woman could or would fix me. In the first three-and-a-half years of my sobriety, I had seven different romantic relationships, confusing lust for love and codependence for companionship, before I reached a bottom on casual affairs. (Casual affairs are like the neutron bomb; they destroy the people and leave the buildings standing.)

Finally, convinced that casual affairs were not the answer, I went a year-and-a-half without any romantic relationships at all. During that celibate period I learned we can become codependent on other things besides people. In my case I became obsessed with my work and the idea that a successful career could fix me. When that illusion failed, I was "blessed" with another suicidal anxiety depression, and I reached a bottom on the codependent notion that occupational identity could fill that gaping hole inside me.

Over the past twenty-seven years I have had to learn the painful lesson that the same hopeless reality is true of sports, hobbies, and material toys. *Nothing* in this world, no person, place, or thing, is going to give me the *identity* I so desperately seek in order to become a whole person. Only a Power greater than anything on this planet can do that for me, and that Power is God, as I understand God, found through working the 12 Steps.

Every day I must admit I am powerless over my codependence and my life has become unmanageable in the areas of abandonment, rejection, insecurity, paranoia, alienation from others, competitiveness, adversarial relationships, distrust, resentment, anger, and low or no self-esteem. I come to believe a Power greater than myself can restore me to sanity by taking away these defective aspects of my character. I make a decision to turn my codependent symptoms over to the care of God, as I understand God.

I have done a lot of writing (Steps 4 and 10) on my codependent personality, and I have shared what I have found in my writing with others (Steps 5, 9, 10, and 12). Over and over, I become entirely ready to have God remove all of these codependent defects of character, and I humbly ask Him to remove my codependent shortcomings.

I have listed all those persons I have harmed with my codependence, and I have tried to make amends wherever possible. I continue to inventory my codependent behavior and to seek through prayer and meditation to find God's will for me with respect to my codependence.

The psychodynamics of codependence lies in what the psychologists call borderline behavior: lack of separation-individuation, splitting good and bad, transference, and loss or distortion of perception of reality. Without going into the scientific details as to how all this works, let me give you an example of just one of my codependent traits in action, and what I did about it by using the 12 Steps.

As a codependent personality I have a rather intense addiction to attention and approval. There is overwhelming evidence that I crave attention and approval like a junkie craves smack. And conversely I am extremely sensitive to lack of attention or lack of approval.

If someone gets attention and I don't, it drives me up the wall. If I get disapproval I want to kill or be killed. Even so the two-sided coin addiction runs rampant here because, just as I'm addicted to attention and approval, I'm also addicted to situations where I get no attention and no approval.

And more often than not, I find myself over and over in situations where I'm getting disapproval, even though this is what I *think* I don't want. How many times in my life have I found myself in situations where I'm getting exactly what I *don't* want? The reason for this is that, believe it or not, I'm *addicted* to it.

I reached my bottom on attention and approval over the past year at the place where I work. In one department I noticed I was obsessing over one woman who ignored me completely and another woman who acknowledged my existence about ten percent of the time and ignored me the rest.

That's the way it was with my mother. Most of the time she ignored me. In another department I obsessed over a woman (my supervisor) who gave most of her approval to others and another woman who never even said hello or good-bye to me. My mother treated others royally and me like a damaged kitchen pot.

I can't tell you how many hours of psychic pain I suffered in these two departments, waiting for those four women to give me attention and approval. And the number of times I went home disappointed – mentally, emotionally, and physically crushed!

I tried everything: being extra nice, complimenting them,

jumping up and down, standing on my head, working harder and faster, wearing nicer clothes, getting a haircut. Nothing worked. I even tried ignoring *them*, acting as though they weren't there, disapproving of them, everything. Nothing I did got them to change their behavior and to give me the attention and approval I craved so desperately.

At home nights and over the weekends I obsessed for hours over these four women. I replayed scenes in my head where they ignored me and gave their attention and approval to others. I enacted scenarios in which I became a rich and famous movie star, finally gaining their attention and approval. I imagined large lawn parties I would throw for big and important people, and I would *not* invite those four women, causing them to wallow in the same agony of rejection I felt when they did not give me their attention and approval at work.

I knew the psychology of the situation involved transference, that the four women were treating me like my mother had treated me, and that I was experiencing the same repressed and unresolved conflicts and rage I had as a child. But no amount of psychological understanding seemed to give me any relief.

These obsessive tape loops on the four women replayed for days, weeks, and months before I began to realize that what I was dealing with was an addiction, and that no amount of knowledge, psychological or otherwise, was going to free me from the bondage of this addiction. I was going to have to work the 12 Steps in order to become liberated.

I used the 2nd, 4th, 5th, 10th, and 11th Steps to give a name to this addiction. At first I didn't know *what* to call it. Immaturity? Grandiosity? Over-Sensitivity? Fear of rejection? All of these defective personality traits of mine were certainly present in the experiences with the four women. But what was it exactly that I wanted from them?

I tried coming to believe that a Power greater than myself

could restore me to sanity. I wrote about the experiences with the four women. I shared my writing with others at meetings and on the telephone. Some people gave me feedback. Some of the feedback was helpful and provided me with clues as to what was going on.

I designated a part of my mind as a continual "10th Step-Taker," an area of my thought that acted as a constant *observer*, taking a moment-to-moment inventory on an on-going basis. Whenever I felt those intense feelings of fear, anger, shame, and guilt around the four women because of the way they were treating me, I asked myself right away what it was that I wanted from them.

In my morning and afternoon meditations, I prayed for knowledge of God's will for me in the situation with the four women. It took me several months to derive that it was "attention and approval" I so desperately craved, and once I had names for the addiction I was able to work the remaining 1st, 3rd, 6th, 7th, 8th, 9th, and 12th Steps on it. In this way I slowly began to experience a serenity and a joy around those four women and around anyone else who didn't give me the attention and approval I so helplessly needed.

Everyone needs attention and approval. Everyone dislikes abandonment and rejection and experiences a certain amount of insecurity, paranoia, and alienation from time to time. We all have a degree of competitiveness, distrust, and low self-esteem. It's only natural. And it's only natural to desire healthy interdependent relationships with other human beings. We might even develop a loving and mutually exclusive companionship with one person that might even turn into marriage. It's important to be able to distinguish between interdependence and codependence.

You and you alone can determine whether your behavior is interdependent (healthy) or codependent (addictive). Only you can tell if your relationship with your significant other is healthy or addictive. I use "size" and "time" as measuring sticks.

If someone ignores me and the pain lasts up to five minutes, I consider that healthy. If I obsess over it all weekend, I call that addictive. When I wonder sometimes if people like me, I would call that healthy. But if I go around all day long wallowing in self-doubt, paranoia, and low self-esteem wondering whether people like me, I would say that's pretty addictive and pretty typical of codependent thinking.

If my spouse and I are mutually supportive and enjoy each other's love and companionship, that looks like an interdependent and healthy relationship. If we hang onto each other's words and deeds, ever clinging, always concerned, and generally obsessive over what the other is doing, it sounds like the addiction of codependence is in full bloom.

Obviously there are many spaces between the two extremes. Only you can determine what space you're actually in. My motive for determining if something is healthy or addictive is not ethical or medical or even entertaining. It's strictly self-preservation.

I've found that in order for me to live a healthy happy life I have to *treat* the many addictive behaviors I've developed over the years. In order for me to treat those addictions, I have to know whether or not I'm practicing them. Once I determine that, I can choose either to do something about it or not. Doing something about it for me means working the 12 Steps as quickly as possible. It's less painful that way.

Several years ago I was on vacation away from home, sitting on a friend's couch in his living room, and there was no one to "play" with and nothing to do. All my friends were busy and that empty, helpless, hopeless feeling was beginning to crawl all over my skin and into my chest and stomach.

As I sat on the couch with all kinds of things in front of me (my journal, a chess game in progress, my writing, three kinds of books to read), I became aware of just how thoroughly dependent I am on other people for my own amusement. I felt I could not do anything by myself. I needed *someone* else to be with me. It was as though I was not even inside my own body. My being had no existence without the interaction of another human being to validate me.

This phenomenon of not being able to be on my own, of not feeling comfortable inside my own skin, is at the bottom of *all* my addictions, tangible and intangible. I seek through outside substances, things, people, and experiences to have something to fill up my empty insides. And nothing ever works for very long except the God I have found through working the 12 Steps and going to the 12-Step meetings.

The importance of the 12-Step meetings and fellowships cannot be emphasized enough. They provide a place where I can spread my neediness for attention, love, and support over a large number of people. History has shown that wives, children, and close friends have never been able to provide the length and breadth of attention, love, and support I need for even one day, let alone a lifetime. The times that I've looked to one woman to fill such demands always ended in tragedy.

In the 12-Step programs of Al-Anon, Adult Children of Alcoholics, Co-Dependents Anonymous, and The 12 Steps for Everybody we find the great numbers of loving and supportive fellow codependents we need to understand us. They are able to love us until we can learn to love ourselves.

With the help of these 12-Step groups we can learn to give up our destructive codependent addictions to people, places, and things and to form constructive, interdependent, and truly happy relationships.

Chapter 8

SEX

The study of addiction becomes more and more fascinating to me as time goes by. Addiction is a disease that usually tells us we don't even have it. It's a disease that often creates great shame and embarrassment. It's a disease that frequently hides itself in dishonesty. For these reasons alone addiction presents a great challenge. It throws up roadblocks and *dares* us to get well.

One of the roadblocks to "recovery" is dishonesty. To paraphrase one of the 12-Step programs, "some of us are sicker than others, but we have a chance to get well if we can be honest." In the long run I would say the best way to deal with the question of sex is to be as honest as possible and to tell the truth.

I first discovered the orgasmic pleasure of genital stimulation while shinning up a lamppost when I was ten years-old. A thrilling tingling sensation spread throughout my whole body. I didn't know what it was. At first I thought I was having some kind of mystical experience from God, and I was frightened. Then I realized the lamppost was doing it to me, and I became embarrassed.

I looked surreptitiously around at the houses on the street to see if anyone was watching me through one of the windows. I clung to the top of that lamppost with the tingling pleasure flowing through me and tried to calculate how long it would last and how long I could stay there before someone discovered me and made me slide down.

Interesting the way the ten year-old potential addict's mind operates. First, I discovered something that gave me pleasure. Then, I felt shame and guilt over it. Then, despite the shame and guilt, I tried to figure out how I could do it for as long as possible without being caught and without having to pay the consequences. Before I even finished with the original experience, I knew there were going to be negative consequences.

Sex is a complicated human activity. It includes the act of penetration and ejaculation specifically for the purpose of reproduction, as well as flirting, cuddling, petting, rubbing, and various kinds of physical and mental stimulation, which may or may *not* lead to reproduction.

Non-reproductive sex can have many conscious and unconscious motivations, including love, lust, pleasure, escape, power, anger, fear, revenge, and guilt. There may also be combinations of the above. It can get *very* complicated, but for me from the very beginning I know I used sex as a drug in order to relax and to escape from the bad feelings, to try to fill that hole gaping inside me.

At the age of twelve I discovered masturbation and proceeded to do it whenever I could. At least once a day, sometimes five to eight times, I would find some place to hide and masturbate. Sometimes my penis got so raw it would bleed, and I would develop sores. Sometimes I couldn't refrain from masturbation long enough for the sores to heal.

I knew vaguely I was using masturbation as a means of escape, and I felt guilty about it, but somehow I just couldn't kick the habit. No matter how hard I tried I always went back to it when the pressure of life built up in me.

Then, when I was fifteen and discovered alcohol as a means of escape, I didn't have to masturbate quite as much to fill the hole.

As for women, I was extremely afraid of them and had the idea that sex with a woman was the rottenest and most despicable act you could commit. I thought women hated sex and considered it a filthy habit, invented by men as an infantile means of expressing power. I got this idea from my mother.

In my teens I observed that the women I dated enjoyed hugging and kissing, but when it came to petting or the actual sex act, they avoided it like the plague. I didn't want to force anybody to do anything they didn't want to do, so I turned to prostitutes for my sexual gratification with women. Thus began the more serious negative consequences of my addictive dependence on sex.

In Korea in 1956, the prostitutes carried many venereal diseases, some of which were particularly resistant to antibiotics. I caught gonorrhea three times and two of the strains were quite difficult to bring under control. Complications resulted in prostatitis, non-specific urethritis, seminal vesiculitis, cankers, warts, strictures, and crab lice. I suffered the pain of these physical consequences of my addiction to sex, which we might as well call lust, all the way through my first marriage. But, that didn't keep me away from prostitutes and one-night stands.

There was another negative consequence to my lust, which I hadn't counted on. One of the Korean prostitutes, my steady girlfriend, told me a few months before I left the country that she had aborted a baby by me and had wrapped the fetus in a rag and thrown it into a garbage dumpster.

Up until then I'd always thought I was a pretty "cool" guy when it came to namby-pamby things like babies, but when I heard what happened to my *own* baby, the bottom dropped right out of my stomach. I thought about that dead baby for weeks; I couldn't get it out of my head.

I didn't realize at the time, however, that it was my addiction to sex, my lust, that had caused that baby's pain and death. Nor did I realize it would be many years and many victims later before I would stop using sex as a means of escape from the stress of life. Thus began the mental, emotional, and spiritual consequences of my addiction to sex.

Before going further let me explain what I believe is the

difference between "healthy" and "addictive" sexual desire. Healthy sexual desire is any feeling that results in loving and constructive behavior. Addictive sexual desire or lust is any feeling that results in selfish and destructive behavior. The difference is plain to see.

For a long time I made a socio-political issue out of my lust. I told myself that sexual guilt and repression were ethically wrong and that total sexual freedom and expression were not only right, they were my *political duty*.

To use as many four-letter words as I chose, to masturbate as often as I liked, and to have intercourse with as many married and unmarried women as I could was my way of defending my right to life, liberty, and the pursuit of happiness. I was a national hero when it came to lust, a legend in my own mind.

It didn't matter how many women I hurt or how many unborn babies I killed, I had a larger cause to perform. It was a pretty fancy denial system for something that turned out to be just another sick addiction.

I believe we can always test any behavior in these terms. If we *have* to do it, no matter who gets hurt, the chances are it's an addiction. And sooner or later there's usually a heavy price to pay for practicing sex or anything else as an addiction.

In my twenties and thirties I became a ladies' man of sorts. I was never a *real* ladies' man. I was always too resentful and fearful of women. But with the help of alcohol and drugs I managed to have many girlfriends, two marriages, and several romantic affairs covering a thirty-year period, before I met my present wife twenty-three years ago.

I was sort of proud of myself. Wasn't that what a real man was supposed to do, have lots of women? That's what society smiled on. Modern movies, books, and music extolled the virtues of the *macho* man. Who needed love? I had sex, drugs, and rock 'n roll!

At thirty-five I met and married my second wife. This was

the first time in my own mind that I experienced anything *remotely* resembling love. It turned out to be mostly lust, envy, and codependence, but at the time I thought it was true love. At the time I was *incapable* of *true* love.

Of *real* love, which is that feeling of *unconditional* affection, benevolence, and compassion toward other human beings, I knew nothing and would know nothing until I had been in the 12-Step programs for four-and-a-half years.

My love for my second wife was predicated upon her willingness and ability to give me attention, companionship, emotional support, adoration, and sex. These were the things my ego/identity so desperately needed from her in order to survive.

In my second marriage I began to confuse lust with love, and from then on every time I felt lust for a woman I fell in love. This caused immense social problems in my life; however, God works in mysterious ways, and what often appears to be adversity turns out to be a blessing in disguise. The following painful experience gave me the willingness to pull myself out of the prison of my addiction to sex by working the 12 Steps.

At three-and-a-half years of sobriety I met the woman who was to be my last casual affair. I had been searching for "Ms. Right" ever since I got sober, and this woman was everything I thought would qualify her for the job: attractive, sexy, shy, attentive. I could see she liked me, and so naturally I fell in love on the spot. It wouldn't be real love if it didn't happen like a rifle shot, right?

We took the obligatory week before hopping into bed. Once again I confused sex with intimacy. Real intimacy, *really* getting to know someone, takes years and involves communication and interaction much more complicated than sex. However I was convinced that the most intimate thing you could do with a person was to take their nude body and turn it into a trapeze act. Macho man!

So I wooed this woman and we had a month of wonderful travel, companionship, and sex. I thought, this is "The One"! This is Ms. Right for sure. And then a strange and horrifying thing happened. I lost my sexual desire for her. It happened very quickly. I was afraid of how she would respond to this information, but I knew I had to be honest with her, because I just couldn't bring myself to fake the sex act.

I could see she was confused when I told her I didn't want to make love any more, but she seemed to like me a lot and she tried to adjust to the situation.

Before the end of the second month I lost my desire to be with her completely. It was over for me. No reason. She was still the same attractive, sexy, shy, attentive woman she had been in the beginning. I just didn't want her any longer. She'd become a "used napkin" to me. I'll never forget the look on her face when I told her I didn't want to see her any more. It was the same look I'd seen on my son's face when he was three years-old and sat terrified in the corner, watching me battle it out with his mother in a drunken rage.

Once again my selfish, destructive, addictive behavior had demolished another human being. This was my *bottom* on my addiction to sex.

I made up my mind I was never again going to hurt another human being with my sexual behavior as long as I lived, one day at a time, if it was in my power. And I knew the only way it could be in my power was if I used the 12 Steps on my lust. I felt this was what God wanted me to do, to avoid sex with *any* woman unless I was entirely ready to commit myself to that woman for the rest of my life.

I went for a year-and-a-half without having sex with anyone before I met the woman who has become my present wife. It was a mind-expanding experience. For the first time in my life I learned how to be just *friends* with women. I learned that women are actually human beings, not simply objects to gratify my sexual desire. I began to realize how selfish I had been with women all my life.

Not having sex with the women I dated was very threatening to my male identity. I began to fear for my sexuality, that perhaps I would lose my ability to have sex. By working the 12 Steps and attending 12-Step meetings that dealt with sex addiction, I was able to see that these fears were merely smoke screens of denial.

The mind will come up with any excuse to encourage us to indulge in our addictions. At these times I realized just how powerless I was over sex and just how unmanageable my life had become. To be dependent upon another human being for your own identity or even your own gratification is the worst kind of dependence possible.

By working the 12 Steps on my lust, I was able to take the responsibility for my own sexual gratification, thus liberating me and the woman from sexual bondage. Today, because it is based on love and mutual respect rather than *need*, my sex life is better than it has ever been. No one is getting hurt, because it's *constructive* rather than *destructive*.

Once I had taken the first three Steps on lust, admitting my powerlessness, letting it go, and turning it over, I found Steps 4 and 5 to be particularly useful in *leaving* it turned over. Sexual addiction, like any other, is insidious and will come up with all kinds of reasons why we *should* indulge in it.

Part of my story on sex is so selfish, so destructive, and so embarrassing that I would not share it in print. This doesn't mean, however, that I did not write it out and share it with others on an individual and private basis, making a searching and fearless moral inventory of my sexual behavior and admitting to God, to myself, and to another human being the exact nature of my wrongs.

I firmly believe that those who do not remember the mistakes of their past are doomed to repeat them, and I never want to repeat the sexual mistakes of my past. One of those mistakes has to do with "mutual consent" regarding sex. Somehow I used to feel that if the other person *wanted* to have sex, that made it "all right." I never took into consideration the people who were *not* present who might have been hurt, if they knew what was going on.

In the old days, whether with a wife, a girlfriend, or a complete stranger, I always put my *own* sexual needs first and theirs second. This was especially true when I wanted to *do* it. When I wanted to *do* it, a steam roller couldn't stop me. Some people found this cute, some found it macho, others just couldn't resist. When I look back on it now, I realize it was merely infantile, or adolescent at best.

By working the 12 Steps on sex, I have come to find selfish sexual behavior as both boorish and inhumane. Part of my amends (Steps 8 and 9) to all of those women in the past who I tricked, argued, cajoled, and forced to have sex, is to leave it entirely up to my present wife as to when we do, or don't, have sex. This is called taking the other person into complete consideration.

Today, if my present wife doesn't want to have sex, I assume the personal responsibility for the gratification of my own sexual needs. Today with the on-going help of the 12 Steps I depend on no one else for the gratification of my sexual needs, and this makes my marriage a safe haven for my wife and myself, rather than a sexual battleground. This is one of the positive results of working the 12 Steps on sex.

While I was sexually abstinent from women for a year-and-a-half, the problem of masturbation came up in my life again. Since I didn't have alcohol, drugs, cigarettes, food, and coffee to escape the bad feelings, I found myself once again using masturbation to escape and find relief.

Because masturbation is not so obviously destructive to

ourselves or to others as some other sexual activities, where is the "bottom" and what is the motivation for abstinence or even *moderation* in this sexual arena? For me the answer to this question lies in whether or not a *particular* behavior works, whether or not I can live with the negative consequences.

At the time of my sexual abstinence from women, I was going through another suicidal anxiety-depression. My anxiety level was so great that at times I found it difficult to breathe. I tried masturbation to cut the anxiety, and five minutes later I would be more anxious than ever. Masturbation wasn't working any more.

Like booze, drugs, and all the rest, I had reached that bottom where it wasn't doing for me what it had done in the past. It no longer took away the pain. Instead I was simply left with greater feelings of helplessness, shame, and frustration. The Step 1 experience – powerlessness and unmanageability – was upon me with a vengeance with respect to masturbation.

This does not mean I refrained from masturbation completely. Some 12-Step programs such as Sexaholics Anonymous define sexual abstinence as giving up *all* sexual activity unless it is with a wife or life-partner. I felt I could use the 12-Steps to *moderate* my use of masturbation. I put masturbation in the same category as anger, food, and coffee and defined abstinence as "moderation."

Sex and Love Addicts Anonymous is a 12-Step program that follows a similar type of abstinence. I have found that moderate (unselfish and non-destructive) abstinence works for me in the areas of anger, food, coffee, and masturbation. I am not going to try my theory on alcohol, drugs, or cigarettes, because I do *not* believe it would work on those addictions.

Vigilance, prayer, meditation, and working with others (Steps 10, 11, and 12) are the means by which I continue the positive results in my life today regarding my sexual behavior.

For five years I corresponded by mail with a member of

Sexaholics Anonymous. We have never met. I don't even know what he looks like. But during those five years of writing and mutually sharing our experience, strength, and hope with each other, the wonders of the 12th Step have come to fruition for me.

Today, I no longer have to feel embarrassed by any sexual *thought* I might have, and I no longer have to *act* on inappropriate or addictive sexual thoughts. By attending the 12-Step groups that deal with sex addiction, such as Sexaholics Anonymous, Sex and Love Addicts Anonymous, Sex Addicts Anonymous, as well as The 12 Steps for Everybody, I have learned understanding, forgiveness, acceptance, and love for my fellow men and women.

Instead of wanting to hide my head in the sand, today I am proud to stand up and admit that I am a human being, no longer jerked along by the leash of my sexual addiction. The 12 Steps are available and successful for those who want or need them in their sexual lives today.

Chapter 9

SUGAR

If you've got no complaints about the way sugar is affecting your body, your mind, and your emotions, this chapter is not for you. One premise of this book is that only *you* can really say what's causing you problems and only *you* can decide how much effort you want to put into getting healthy.

If sugar hasn't been a problem in your life, just move right along to Chapter Ten on "Anxiety," and see if that fits. As they say in many of the 12-Step programs, just take what you like and leave the rest.

For me excessive sugar, like food and coffee, has a very definite negative effect on my physical, mental, and emotional well-being. If I'm feeling down, sugar will bring me up, *way up*. Initially, I get a buzz on sugar and then comes the crash. First, I feel good, energetic, and positive. Then, I feel exhausted, sluggish, and negative. The same pattern is actually true for *anything* that gives me a "buzz."

Roller-coastering between these two up-and-down extremes is what large quantities of sugar do for me. In this manner it's remarkably similar to alcohol (made from sugar) and coffee (caffeine) in its ability to stimulate, and then to depress. Getting high and then getting hung over was a way of life for me for twenty-seven years with respect to alcohol, drugs, cigarettes, and coffee, and so it was no surprise to me when I discovered I'd been using sugar for the same purpose.

Sugar is processed by three different metabolic systems in the body, and when any one of these goes haywire because of natural causes or misuse, the results can be physically, mentally, and emotionally devastating. Hypoglycemia, diabetes, and even the "phenomenon of craving" can most definitely be attributed to faulty metabolic systems.

The effects often result in erratic mood swings, anxiety, depression, suicidal ideation, paranoia, and certain physical disabilities. When the body cannot adequately process excessive alcohol, drugs, nicotine, coffee, or sugar, the results are usually quite destructive for the individual and for those around him or her.

It took quite a while for me to see what excessive sugar was doing to my mind and emotions. To some degree I still haven't quite reached my bottom on sugar.

My first experiment in giving up sugar was really an attempt to control my food intake and my weight. I decided to abstain from all cookies, candy, cake, or pie, because I felt if I could designate exactly what types of food I was avoiding, I could gain more "control" over my food intake.

I knew cookies, candy, cake, and pie had lots of sugar in them, and I could see when I ate just *one* of any of them, it set up an insatiable craving in me to eat more, until I gorged myself and became physically sick. I was aware of how my life had become unmanageable due to overweight, but I was not aware of how my life had become unmanageable due to the *erratic thinking* and *emotional mood swings* that come from eating excessive sugar.

It so happens when I made myself the promise to give up cookies, candy, cake, and pie, I somehow conveniently neglected to put ice cream on the list. One of my main fixes in sobriety has been choco-chocolate chip ice cream. I love it more than life itself. You can hang me up by my thumbs and flay me with barbed wire; just don't take away my daily ration of choco-chocolate chip ice cream.

When I was five years clean and sober, I got into the habit of buying a pint of choco-chocolate chip ice cream every night and eating it just before I went to bed. From working the 12 Steps on a daily basis, I had become as spiritual as a Hindu yogi, and yet if you tried to take away my pint of choco-chocolate chip ice cream I'd probably put a bullet in your brain, or mine.

Sometimes during 12-Step meetings I would find myself obsessing over the ice cream. I would cut my conversations short with members of the fellowship at the end of the meeting so I could hurry to the store, get my pint of ice cream, and then go home and eat it in isolation and peace.

I felt guilty at the time and even recognized the remarkable similarity of this ice cream eating behavior and my drinking behavior, buying the bottle, hoarding it all to myself, etc., but there seemed nothing I could do about. I was powerless but I wasn't the least bit ready to admit my life had become unmanageable.

In order to maintain my body weight, since one pint of choco-chocolate chip has twelve hundred calories, I had to starve myself during the day. I would eat a puny little breakfast of maybe two hundred calories, a salad for lunch, and a diet TV dinner, and then just before bed I'd gobble down the pint of choco-chocolate chip ice cream. Somehow it didn't seem right, but I'd do it anyway.

Another thing I began to notice was my dreams. They were like high-concept action films with lots of sex and violence! Sometimes in the middle of the night around 4:00 a.m., about six hours after I ate the ice cream, I'd wake up in an "earthquake." It felt like the bed or even the whole room was vibrating like a washing machine.

At first I thought these were spiritual experiences, that my Higher Power was trying to contact me to let me know I was being a good boy by working the 12 Steps and not drinking and using. Then I began to realize that it wasn't the whole room or even the bed that was shaking. It was my body. I had the "shakes," just as if I was coming down off a drunk.

I was getting high from the sugar in the ice cream, just like I'd been getting high from the coffee. At night while I was asleep, I was buzzed. My blood tingled and my dreams filled with wild and crazy things, and then in the early morning I came down and went into withdrawal. And just like the coffee I wasn't sure at first whether I wanted to stop.

It took me two more years to get to the first stopping point, that point where I was finally sick and tired of being sick and tired of the wild dreams and waking up with the shakes. I was ready to have serenity at night, and I knew it was time to work the 12 Steps on that pint of choco-chocolate chip ice cream before bed.

As usual the 12 Steps worked. I gave up the pint of ice cream and gained some physical, mental, and emotional peace in my life at night. But I was not ready to give up sugar entirely. By experimenting with the various types and quantities of food that have sugar, I was able to adopt a level of *moderation*.

It turned out I didn't have to give up ice cream entirely. If I ate one or two scoops of vanilla ice cream once a week, a few hours before I went to bed, I didn't get unmanageable effects from it. Occasionally I could even eat a piece of cake or pie. I could drink one soft drink a day and get away with it. As long as I kept below a certain *daily level* of sugar in my food, I seemed to be all right. It was when I ate *above* that level that the trouble started. I'll give you an example.

One day about seventeen years ago, I had two cups of decaf coffee, two soft drinks, and a pint of chocolate mint ice cream just before I went to sleep. On that particular day I had also neglected my 11th Step meditation in the morning and in the afternoon. The results were predictable.

All night I tossed and turned and came fully awake several times during the night. Inside my head it was as if ten TV sets blared continuously. Dreams, noises, flashbacks, music – all playing at once.

I got up when the alarm went off and tried to sit through my thirty-minute meditation, but it was the same thing. The noises in my mind chattered away. When I finally stood up to do my physical exercises, I was fully aware I was drunk on sugar and my mind was completely out of control.

I made it through the day at work, carefully avoiding the temptation to tell people what I really thought of them and to impulsively slam down the phone on some of the idiotic customers. That night at the 12-Step meeting I began to indulge in my addiction for attention and approval. I became obsessed with one of the women in the meeting that I hated. The obsession lasted twenty-four hours.

Then I came down with an attack of paranoia concerning my wife, which lasted thirty-six hours before it finally left me. This experience shows how a sugar "slip" triggered off *several* of my addictions and created unmanageability in my physical, mental, and emotional life for a total of three days.

Is it worth it? For some reason I still think it is, because believe it or not, I am still not *entirely* ready to give up that occasional pint of choco-chocolate chip.

Just how hard does my bottom have to be on sugar? Do I have to develop sugar diabetes? Do I have to go out and kill somebody while high on sugar? These are questions I cannot answer.

I know there are positive addictions like being on time. There are harmless addictions like cleaning my eyeglasses. There are addictions for which the 12 Steps have provided me with a degree of moderation like coffee. And there are addictions which cause a certain unmanageability in my life, but which haven't yet provided me with the motivation necessary to moderate them completely, like sugar.

There is no doubt I am addicted to sugar. I work the 12 Steps on sugar-eating to the best of my ability, but sometimes I still go on excessive sugar binges. As they say, "it takes what it takes."

I don't believe that *anybody* can give up *anything* unless they are *entirely* ready, and I can't beat myself up if I'm not ready to give up excessive sugar entirely. Instead, I pray for my Higher Power's will for me in all areas of my life, including excessive sugar, and I have faith I will be shown what I'm supposed to do, one day at a time.

I know that one can always receive help for their sugar addiction by going to Overeaters Anonymous and 12 Steps for Everybody meetings on a regular basis, when they are ready.

Chapter 10

ANXIETY

My longest-standing addiction is anxiety. I've suffered from it all my life. Early photographs show me sitting in my diaper in an overstuffed chair with a look of sheer terror in my eyes. A friend once described the look as "like piss-holes in the snow."

The dictionary defines *anxiety* as uneasiness, apprehension, or worry. It defines fear as agitation, dread, or fright. Words by any other name would be the same for me. Anxiety or fear is what it is, and I've had it from the moment I was born.

Let me tell you what anxiety feels like to me. The pit of my stomach seems to be falling out. My heart becomes constricted and starts to pound. My lungs feel as if they're in a vise. My chest heaves and I have difficulty in breathing. My pulse and respiration increase and my skin tingles. I often feel as if I'm being immersed in a vat of ice water. I suffer chills and need to put on warmer clothes. I lose the feeling in my hands and feet.

When I'm in anxiety my sense of taste and smell disappears. I often have trouble hearing things properly and my eyesight plays tricks on me. I tend to have auditory and visual hallucinations. My thoughts and emotions become jumbled. My face becomes fixed and immobile, and my eyes begin to bug out. I become dysfunctional and socially inept. I feel as though I'm in tremendous pain, and I want to die.

If a grizzly bear walked into your room right now, you'd probably agree it would be appropriate to experience *some* of the above symptoms, but my symptoms have been with me from my earliest memories up until twenty-three years ago, and there has been no reason at all – no life-threatening situation, no physical or mental attack, no obvious danger of any kind. My anxiety is called "free-floating" anxiety by the psychiatrists, and they tend to treat it with tranquilizers.

For twenty-seven years I treated my anxiety with alcohol and drugs, until one day twenty-three years ago with four years of sobriety I learned I was *addicted* to my anxiety, and I could treat it with the 12 Steps.

I started drinking alcoholically when I was fifteen in order to medicate my anxiety. It worked as long as I was drunk. I had no fear when I was drinking. I bought liquor illegally, I stole things, I drove cars ninety miles-an-hour, and I got into fights with bigger and older men. But when the liquor wore off I was afraid of the dark. I was afraid of my own shadow. It made no sense.

For twenty-five years I went to psychiatrists to figure out why I was so afraid. I was convinced the answer lay in the deep dark secrets of my past. I read all the self-help books I could get my hands on. I went back to college and got yet another degree, this time in psychology. I drank more alcohol and took more drugs. Nothing worked.

Meanwhile my life became more and more unmanageable due to anxiety. I was afraid to talk to women. I was afraid of my bosses and my fellow employees. I was afraid of my students, my wives, even my own children. I was afraid to take risks. I was afraid of confrontation. I was afraid of criticism.

I had absolutely no idea what was going on with my anxiety until I came into my first 12-Step program and started working the 12 Steps. Without the aid of alcohol and drugs, I went into a seven-month suicidal anxiety depression because my second ex-wife wouldn't take me back. Then, I had a ten-month suicidal anxiety depression because I couldn't succeed at the business I was in. During these anxiety attacks, every day I begged God to let me die.

How could I be working a good 12-Step program if I was

in such pain? I was going to one, usually *three*, 12-Step meetings a day. I was hauling clients from a halfway house to outside meetings twice a week. I made the coffee at one meeting, the food at another, did the literature at another, and was secretary of another. I was the General Service Representative at still another meeting, and I was the Central Service Representative at another.

I answered phones once every two weeks at one central office and every week at another. I sponsored seven different people in two different programs. I spoke on the telephone every day to at least six or eight program people, and I had a 12-Step mail correspondence going across the country with about twenty people on three different programs. What was wrong with my 12-Step program? Why was I suffering so much anxiety that I wanted to kill myself?

The answer was right there in front of me. One day a guy at a meeting suggested I was getting a *payoff* from the anxiety. He said I ought to do a separate 4th Step inventory on my fears. I was so angry I walked away from him. I just couldn't accept the idea that I was hooked on the anxiety.

It took several more months of excruciating pain before I was willing to take the guy's suggestion. After making a list of some thirty-five separate and distinct fears I was suffering, I became willing to admit I was an anxiety junkie and that my life had become unmanageable.

In this *4th* Step list of fears I discovered I was afraid of losing and afraid of winning. I was afraid of rejection and afraid of acceptance. I was afraid of failure and afraid of success. The two-sided coin phenomenon of my addiction to anxiety was apparent.

It didn't matter *what* the stimulus was, if I was in the market for fear today I'd be afraid of it. I also discovered it was useless to try to figure out *why* I was afraid of all these things. You could blame it on my genes, my glands, or my mother. It didn't matter. Since it was an addiction, understanding wouldn't help. But, I knew that working the 12 Steps would.

Examining my list of thirty-five fears, which the psychiatrists had labeled free-floating anxiety, I was able to see how each separate fear was an addiction in itself. If my addiction to anxiety was a cluster of thirty-five separate little addictive fears, I could work the 12 Steps on them taken together or individually. Either way, it didn't matter.

It was easy to observe the payoffs for each individual fear. When I indulged in fear of losing and somehow conveniently lost in games, work, and love over and over again, I could treat myself to self-pity, guilt, inferiority, and self-punishment. And then I could get angry and beat myself over the head with my failure.

When I indulged in fear of winning, whenever I got close to some form of success, I could treat myself to guilt (it will hurt the other person if I beat him), fear of retaliation (the losers will be angry with me), self-doubt and irresponsibility (I'm not strong enough to be a winner), and performance anxiety (I won't be able to *keep on* winning).

If I experienced rejection anxiety, the payoffs were anger, arrogance, withdrawal, isolation, and righteous rejection of the other person.

If I felt "acceptance" anxiety, the payoffs were "I'm not good enough," "I'll never be able to do it again," and "I'll never be able to *keep* it, whatever it is." I was getting a lot of "payoff" mileage out of my fears.

Many of the payoffs for free-floating anxiety are the same as those discussed in Chapters 3 and 5 on Anger and Family Members. Anxiety gives us that adrenaline rush which comes with being afraid. We get a fix from adrenaline.

We get sympathy and attention from others when we're suffering an anxiety attack. Attention is something we always crave and never get enough of. Anxiety gives us a good excuse for not getting down to business and doing what we're supposed to do. We might even call in sick. This allows us to indulge in sloth. It also gives us control over our environment and other people.

Anxiety keeps us emotionally busy so we don't have to feel other uncomfortable emotions like anger, shame, guilt, envy, or boredom. Boredom is one of the most painful feelings I have to deal with, though I often don't recognize it as such. I've given up businesses, jobs, friendships, and marriages because I was bored.

Recently I sat through three horror films in a row becoming so frightened I couldn't sleep, simply because I didn't have anything "better" to do. Today I call that a good example of indulging in my addiction to anxiety.

The fact is my body is habituated to anxiety. I have a neurological craving to be frightened, and from time to time I go out of my way to indulge in this addiction to fear, putting myself in fearful situations despite the pain it causes me. This is the addict's desire to satisfy the nervous system's yearning for that which both *fixes* us and *screws us up* at the same time.

Booze, drugs, cigarettes, anger, food, family members, it's all the same to us. What we do not handle well, we also crave. Pass the anxiety, please.

I began working the 12 Steps on anxiety when I became sick and tired of being sick and tired of the pain it caused me. Once I started recognizing anxiety for what it is, an addiction in its own right, I became less and less able to get away with it.

Once the drinker learns his drinking is a disease and he is powerless over it, it ruins his drinking for the rest of his life. I admitted I was powerless over anxiety and that my life had become unmanageable. I came to believe a Power greater than myself could restore me to sanity and take away my anxiety. I made a decision to turn my will, my life, and my anxiety over to the care of God, as I understood God.

I didn't experience *complete* relief from anxiety right away. It came and went. It was worse in the morning and seemed to fade away in the afternoon. At night I would be anxiety-free. The next morning the “grizzly bear” would be sitting on my chest again.

I continued doing more 4th and 10th Step inventory writing on my anxiety, and I worked the 6th and 7th Steps daily, humbly asking God to remove this shortcoming, if it was God’s will for me. I worked the 8th, 9th, and 12th Steps by sharing my experience, strength, and hope with others who I perceived to be having difficulty with anxiety, if they showed an interest in hearing what I had to say. I talked on the phone with one person almost daily for four years, listening patiently to his sharing on his anxiety and giving him support in working the 12 Steps on it.

Perhaps the most dramatic single experience I've had working any *one* of the 12 Steps on any *one* of my addictions is the miraculous way my chronic anxiety responded to Step 11: "Sought through prayer and meditation to improve our conscious contact with God *as we understood Him*, praying only for knowledge of His will for us and the power to carry that out."

Having dabbled unsuccessfully in prayer and meditation for the first five years of my sobriety, it took that second suicidal anxiety depression to bring me to my knees with respect to the 11th Step.

The idea of daily meditation was a big bore to me. I simply didn't have *time* for it. When I did "sit" in the morning for ten minutes or so, my mind became a beehive of thoughts and noises, which far from resembled anything like the joy and serenity that meditation was supposed to bring.

But driven by the agonies of my suicidal anxiety attacks, I kept meditating in the morning, extending it from ten to twenty minutes, and slowly the mind chatter began to dissipate and

I received moments, or rather seconds, of mental and emotional peace.

I also noticed that after my morning meditations, while I was brushing my teeth and shaving, I got messages in my mind, the answers to certain questions and problems which didn't seem to be coming from my own brain, but rather from some "outside source."

With a mental health history like mine, there was always the possibility that these "spiritual revelations" were just hallucinations or delusions, but I preferred to think of them as communications from my Higher Power. I was beginning to understand God, not only as a Power that kept me from drinking and as a refuge from my anxiety, but also as a source of *guidance*. The 11th Step gave me a sense of well-being and a feeling that all's right with the world and there's nothing to worry about.

And then one morning in April of 1984, a wonderful thing happened. I'll never forget it, because it has meant so much to me for the past twenty-two years. I arose and headed for the couch where I regularly meditated, hoping that the killer anxiety attack would not come upon me. I sat down, placed the backs of my hands on the tops of my thighs, closed my eyes, and focused on my breath as it went in and out at the tip of my nose.

My mind was its usual jumble of mixed feelings and chattering thoughts, and then I sensed the presence of that painful all-pervading anxiety depression, the constricted chest, the freezing extremities, the difficulty in breathing, and the suicidal low self-esteem just waiting to take over me.

It struggled to get my attention. It demanded of me that I "let it in." Suddenly the thought occurred to me that I didn't have to let it in, if I didn't want to. Out of nowhere the message came to me that I didn't have to experience that overwhelming anxiety any longer, that it was an *addiction*, and that

I didn't *have* to indulge in it any more. *I could choose not to take that first drink of anxiety.*

This revelation blew my mind! As I sat there in the meditation, one part of my mind struggled to indulge in the anxiety while another part said, "No, you don't have to if you don't want to." I could go ahead and take that first drink of fear, which leads to the next and the next and the next. Or I could *refuse* that first drink of fear and stay *sober* from my anxiety. That day in April of 1984 I chose *not* to indulge any longer in excessive anxiety and, one day at a time, I've been choosing not to ever since.

I don't believe I could have made that choice to refuse anxiety one moment earlier than I did. I believe it took every minute of those 47 years and 355 days of anxiety to get me to that place where I was ready to let go of it.

And I believe when we *fully* admit we are powerless over something, *anything*, and that it has made our lives truly *unmanageable*, a condition arises within us that makes us ready and willing to *let go* and *surrender* that addiction completely. When we get to that "pitiful and incomprehensible" point, and then work the *rest* of the 12 Steps on that particular addiction, we gain the *power* to choose *not* to indulge in that addiction, one day at a time. So by admitting our powerlessness and working the 12 Steps, we actually become *powerful*, powerful in a way that was totally impossible for us up to that moment.

Along with the 11th Step, it is important to go to the 12-Step meetings, which apply themselves to working the 12 Steps on such addictions as excessive anxiety. These are Emotions Anonymous, Emotional Health Anonymous, and The 12 Steps for Everybody. Here one can find the fellowship one needs to let go of anxiety and to choose serenity and peace of mind on a daily basis.

The 11th Step is a very necessary tool for me in maintaining the power of choice over my addictions. If I do not work it every day, I find I lose that power of choice and become powerless over my addictions once again.

Today I pray that I choose the 12 Steps and work them in all areas of my life, so that I no longer have to live under the thumb of my addictions.

Chapter 11

DEPRESSION

I used to think it was impossible to be both anxious and depressed at the same time, but when I went through my two suicidal anxiety depressions I found I was wrong. You can suffer anxiety and depression together, and together they can make your life almost unbearable. The psychiatrists call it "agitated depression," but whatever you call it, it does respond to the 12 Steps.

Anxiety for me usually centers around a feeling of physical nervousness, while depression promotes the idea that I'm no good, never was, never will be. Life is the pits. Is this all there is? It's not going to get any better. I might as well be dead. I think I'll go out in the garden and eat worms.

When I drank alcoholically I used to sing these blues until everybody around was ready to shoot me. I'd be happy until about the eighth drink and then I'd become miserable. I had all kinds of reasons why the world was going to hell in a handbasket. I blamed my wife, my kids, my neighbors, my boss, and the President of the United States. They were no damned good. It was no use. There was no hope.

Another aspect to my depression was the two-sided coin phenomenon in which I was attracted to other depression addicts. There was nothing better than finding someone else to help me cry in my beer. Chronic depressives show themselves by the dark shadows under their eyes, the stolid stare, the grim lips.

Whenever I saw a woman with that expression, it was love at first sight. I couldn't wait to get it on, so we could make the perfunctory little efforts to get each other out of our depressions and then settle down to some really good *mutual* commiseration. It was my duty, my karma! It was better than sex.

Somebody once said depression is anger turned inward. I identified with that. I was so filled with repressed anger, if you touched me I went off like a bomb. I grew up believing I wasn't supposed to get angry and if I did I was a bad person, so I did a "slow burn" for forty-three years, and it came out in the form of depression.

I wasn't aware of this until I was a year and a half sober and my second ex-wife wouldn't take me back. During that first suicidal agitated depression there were many times when I couldn't even drag myself out of bed, so I slept all day long. I would pull the covers up over my head and wallow in depressive dreams, one after the other, in which the world was crashing down around me, and I was to blame.

I was so depressed I was unemployable. I finally got a job mowing lawns and was fired the first day because I didn't have the concentration to make the lawn mower go in a straight line. I could barely do my own grocery shopping. I lived two blocks from the supermarket and on the way home carrying the grocery bag, I'd pray to God for the strength to keep from collapsing on the sidewalk. When the depression lifted, I was back to running three miles a day.

The second suicidal anxiety depression, when I was four and a half years sober, gave me a painful look at just how low my self-esteem and self-worth really were. Every day I would beat myself up unmercifully for being a complete failure in work, in life, and as a human being. There was no valid reason I could see for my continuing to live. The depression seemed to feed on these negative attitudes toward myself.

The payoffs for my depression were much the same as those for anger and anxiety. Depression kept me emotionally occupied so I didn't have to feel anger, fear, lust, guilt, or boredom.

Depression got me attention, sympathy, power, and control. There was drama, righteousness, and self-pity available in depression. I could put on a Muddy Waters, Howlin' Wolf, or Leadbelly record and just sing those blues until the tears rolled down my cheeks like little rivers.

I got a lot of self-punishment out of depression. I could assuage my chronic guilt. Grief became a way of life. I grieved over all those things I had lost in my life, and then I came up with a hundred reasons why I would never get them back.

There was something almost *sweet* about the misery generated by my depression. It reminded me of all those sad love stories my mother took me to see in the movie theaters back in the forties when I was a kid. We'd sit in that dark theater for hours and cry until we couldn't cry any more. We were depression junkies together and misery loves company.

My bottom on depression came hand in hand with my bottom on anxiety in my fifth year of sobriety. By working the 10th Step I could see more and more when I was indulging in depression and when I wasn't. The depressions came in the morning when I was alone with my own head and lifted in the afternoon and evening, when I became more actively involved in working with others.

My head was my own worst enemy. I had heard it said in 12-Step meetings: "You can *live* your way into a new way of thinking, but you can't *think* your way into a new way of living."

All that happened when I tried to *think* my way out of the depression was that my head came up with more and more rationalizations for why I should indulge in it. The depression did the thinking for me. I was in a bed of quicksand. The more I struggled with the depression, the deeper I sank.

It became more and more obvious that the way out of the depression was not "thinking" but "action." Taking action is the key to the 12-Step programs. There's the action of *admission* when we admit we are powerless over depression and that our lives have become unmanageable. There's the action of *belief* when we come to believe that a Power greater than ourselves can relieve us of our depression. There's the action of *decision* when we make the decision to turn our will, our life, and our depression over to the care of God, as we understand God.

There's the action of *discovery* when we make a searching and fearless moral inventory of our depression and our depressive behavior. There's the action of *disclosure* when we admit to God, to ourselves, and to another human being the exact nature of our depression. And there's the action of *forgiveness*, which we practice as an integral part of Steps 4 and 5.

Forgiveness is an action I have to take on a daily, sometimes moment-to-moment, basis in order to free myself of the rage, resentment, and guilt that is the food of my depression. If I don't forgive myself and everyone else for everything, my depression feeds on my rage, resentment, and guilt, and I start beating myself up again, stuck smack in the middle of the depression and sinking fast.

Steps 6, 7, 8, and 9 involve the actions of *readiness*, *prayer*, *listing*, and *restitution*. We have to maintain a state of willing readiness for the removal of the depression, or else it won't be removed. For me this readiness means constantly reminding myself of how painful the depression is and how miserable my life becomes if I choose to indulge in it.

I have to humbly pray on a continual basis that the depression be removed. I have to list the people and institutions that I have harmed by my depressions, and I have to make some type of amends for that harm. One way of making amends is by treating people, places, and institutions with acceptance and forgiveness. In this way I create a depression-free atmosphere inside my own head.

The last three Steps, 10, 11, and 12, involve the continuous actions of *inventory*, *evaluation*, *prayer*, *meditation*, *disclosure*, and *right action*. I keep a watchful eye out for depression, and as soon as I see myself indulging in it I admit it's wrong for me to do so.

The depression is going to tell me it's right. It always has a hundred reasons why I *should* be depressed. I had to finally reach the point where depression was *never* an option, no matter what. Certainly it was all right for me to be disappointed from time to time, but depressed, no. The price was too high in pain and suffering. It never did any good being depressed. It never changed anything for the better.

I have tremendous gratitude for the action of the 10th Step: "Continued to take personal inventory and when we were wrong promptly admitted it," because it gives me the ammunition I need to choose not to be depressed. If I don't observe, and inventory, exactly what my mind is doing on a moment-to-moment basis, it slips back into depression in the blink of an eye. Step 10 can be worked in a variety of ways.

Some people take a personal inventory only once a year, making a list of what they're doing right and wrong so they can strive for improvement in certain areas. Others take an inventory once a month or once a week. There's a page in the 12-Step literature which suggests taking an inventory every night just before we go to bed, giving ourselves credit for what we've done right that day and making note of what we might try to change for the better tomorrow.

After trying all of the above, I came to the conclusion that I need to take Step 10 on an on-going basis throughout the day. Otherwise my mind gets me into a lot of trouble very quickly. I can be in the middle of a resentment toward someone, an obsession for food or sex, an anxiety attack, or a depression before I know it. Then getting out of the addiction is much more difficult.

The best way to stay out of an addiction is to nip it in the bud with a continuous Step 10. How is it possible to inventory our thoughts, feelings, and behavior all the time? Where's the time for anything else? The answer lies in a technique I learned while trying to stay out of my suicidal anxiety depressions.

I designated a part of my mind to watch what's going on in the rest of my mind and to "sound the alarm" when it sees something that might create a problem. I call it my 10th Step Mind (my "observer" mind) and with it I monitor my own thoughts, feelings, and behavior on an ongoing basis. Whenever I observe a depressive thought, an excessively anxious feeling, or any other addictive behavior, I promptly admit I'm "wrong" and stop it.

It's only human to be depressed from time to time and so my 10th Step Mind has to make an evaluation right away. Is this depressive thinking something I want to *continue* doing? Is it excessive? Is it doing me any good? Is it helping me to change anything for the better?

By the time it takes to answer these questions, I've usually come to the conclusion that I'm wrong and I'm ready and willing to stop it. The process is simple, but it's not easy. It takes a great deal of practice to utilize the 10th Step on an ongoing basis, but if you're anything like me the pain of the alternative will motivate you to do it.

As I drive my car, walk down the street, or sit at my desk, my mind just naturally seeks something to get angry about, a childhood memory to resent, a sexually stimulating fantasy, a projected fear, or a depressing thought. I can't help myself. I'm addicted to this type of thinking behavior. Those of you who identify and know the pain of this kind of addiction will be motivated to work the 10th Step on a continuous basis.

Today my life is so much better without addictive depression; it's like a dream. Working the 10th Step moment-to-moment I'm able to identify depressive thoughts the minute they arise. As soon as I see one of these "I'm no good," "What's the use?" "Life's the pits!" types of thought creeping into my consciousness, I blow the whistle on it. I'm already determined I will not take a "drink" of that kind of thinking any more, because one drink of depressive thinking only leads to another and another and another.

If I have my 10th Step Mind turned on, depressive thoughts don't get very far before I trap them and chase them out of my mind with the rest of the 12 Steps, admitting I am powerless, coming to believe, making the decision, and so forth. As long as I'm working the 10th Step continuously, depressive thinking has no place in my mind today.

I have to practice Step 11, prayer and meditation, daily in order to stay out of depression. My morning meditations give me a feeling of peace and a sense of well-being that take the place of the painful feelings and distressing thoughts, which go along with depression. In my meditations I know I am all right just the way I am and that there's no real reason to feel insecure, inadequate, or negative.

Step 12 provides the action of working with others who are depressed and sharing my experience, strength, and hope with them so that they, too, can learn to work the 12 Steps on depression and let go of it for good.

Working with others drives out the depressive thoughts, as we become less self-centered and more concerned with those around us. Without addictive depressive thoughts cluttering my mind, there is now plenty of room for happy joyous thoughts and comfortable feelings of well-being.

At first happiness was a problem. I was so used to gloom and doom I thought I wasn't *supposed* to be happy. My mind was habituated to misery. Happiness was a foreign element. Today I know it's all right for me to be content with my life and with myself as an individual. With the help of the 12 Steps my mind today is generally filled with contentment.

Today there are 12-Step groups like Emotions Anonymous, Emotional Health Anonymous, and The 12 Steps for Everybody that hold meetings for people who are ready to let go of their depression. Recovering people share their 12-Step experience, strength, and hope with those who are willing to listen.

If they're not interested and seem bent upon pursuing their depression, they are free to continue with it. It's not possible for anyone to convince others that they have an addictive problem with depression. It's only possible for the person who is really *ready* to work the 12 Steps on their depression and to let go of it one day at a time.

Chapter 12

NEGATIVE THINKING

Despite its similarity to depression, negative thinking is very much an addiction in its own right. My mind has tended to think negatively rather than positively for as long as I can remember, but I had no idea up until twenty-three years ago it was an addiction. I was under the mistaken impression that the negative thoughts, which flowed through my head all day, were actually part of a *valid* point of view, instead of an addictive *distortion* of reality.

I've always been very good at gathering the evidence to support a negative point of view. After all, if it's raining outside it's got to be a miserable day. It doesn't matter that I'm enjoying my work, and I just got a raise. It's raining! If the service is slow, it's a lousy restaurant. The food, the decor, and the company might be good, but don't you see, the service is bad! That's the way my mind naturally works: very one-sided, very narrow, and very negative.

The other side of the coin, *hearing* negative things from other negative people, was also something I was hooked on. My tendency was to ask a person how they were doing, and then to sit back and listen to the tragedy unfold. I thought it was my duty to *listen* to other people's negative thinking. What's a friend for but to sit there and soak up hour after hour of negative remarks? It gave my own negative thinking something to feed on.

If I didn't have anything traumatic to report, I didn't feel there was anything worthwhile to talk about. I was afraid the other person would get bored if I talked positive. I thought people who talked positive were either insincere or just plain unrealistic.

Didn't they understand how *miserable* life really was? The

friends I chose were equally negative. We'd all sit around and criticize the government, big business, our bosses, our fellow employees, our neighbors, and any of our friends who weren't there to defend themselves.

Our favorite target for criticism was the President of the United States. When all else failed we always got a kick out of putting down the President. We were iconoclasts. We loved tearing things down and we were proud of it. Building things up was not part of our behavior pattern.

I carried this same practice right into my first 12-Step program. For the first five years I found 12-Step meetings where I could dump all my negativity with impunity, and then dutifully sat back and listen while others did the same. Most of us were negative thinking junkies and didn't even know it.

There's a good excuse for my addiction to negative thinking. I grew up in a family where negativity was an avocation as well as a way of life. On my mother's side they were devout practitioners of negative thinking, criticism, and dire predictions.

On my father's side they were into judgmentalism, opinionism, and worry. While my mother and her family were busy grieving over the past, criticizing everything in sight, and predicting the end of the world, my father and his family were judging everything that moved, giving their opinions about everything, and worrying about it all.

You can imagine how much fun we had at family gatherings! Is it any wonder I became addicted to negative thinking and its various forms, including criticism, judgmentalism, and pessimism?

Besides the basic *payoff* for negative thinking – the positive reinforcement I got from my family who modeled it for me – there's a long list of additional payoffs. Negative thinking keeps my mind busy with *thoughts*, so I don't have to feel *feelings*. Most addicts will go to any lengths to avoid feeling feelings, even if it means being so completely occupied with negative thoughts that it's detrimental to our physical, mental, and emotional health.

It seems easier for us to cope with negative, pessimistic, destructive, critical, judgmental ideas and opinions than it is for us to cope with anger, fear, joy, and even contentment. "Thoughts are less painful than feelings," says the typical addict.

Aside from the need to escape feelings, we addictive personalities have a strong wish to escape the "here-and-now." For some strange reason the *present* is quite painful for us, and so we slide back into the *past* or up into the *future* in order to avoid the present.

Negative thinking is the perfect way to escape the present. The past and the future hold an unlimited source of incidents, real and imaginary, over which we can practice criticism, judgment, and pessimism. What better way to avoid facing today's problems than to mull over yesterday's or tomorrow's? And what better way to avoid accepting *our part* in today's problems than by judging and criticizing the behavior of others, so we can continue to avoid judging or criticizing our own?

When all else fails we turn our judging, criticizing minds onto ourselves. Thus we expend *all* our energy on negative thinking and *none* on positive change. Most negative thinking addicts rarely have positive solutions to contribute. Positive solutions don't feed our addiction to negative thinking, and so they have no use for us.

"Opinionism" is one way I feed my negative thinking addiction. I tend to have an opinion on everything. Just ask me and I'll give it to you. Along with each opinion is an expectation, sometimes many expectations, regarding the way I think people, places, and things ought to behave.

Holding as many opinions and expectations as I do gives me the right to *judge* and *criticize* everything, especially if my opinions and expectations are not met. Since I'm a perfectionist, *nothing* ever satisfies my opinions or expectations. This gives me a tremendous sense of righteous indignation. Thus, I justify holding a tremendous resentment against the entire universe.

Opinionism allows me always to be dissatisfied with the way people, places, and thing are, and to indulge in as much negative thinking as I can fit into any given day. It all works perfectly to support my addiction to negative thinking.

I started to reach my bottom on negative thinking five years ago in the middle of my second suicidal depression, when it occurred to me one day that my negative, judgmental, critical mind was eating me alive. I was like a wounded dog that was feeding on its own bowels.

It wasn't enough for me any more just to judge and criticize others; I had to annihilate *myself* daily with relentlessly critical opinions in order to satisfy my addiction for negative thinking. I was the judge, jury, prosecutor, and defendant all rolled into one, and I orchestrated it all inside my own head. It became clear to me that most of the pain I suffered from my suicidal depression was caused by *me*, and *I* was getting sick and tired of being sick and tired of negative thinking.

I reviewed my past and realized I had been my own worst enemy and if anybody else had treated me the way I treated myself over the years, I would've probably had them shot. Nobody had judged and criticized *me* more harshly than *I* had. My addiction to negative thinking was destroying me! I was finally ready to admit I was powerless over negative thinking and my life had become unmanageable.

And if a Power greater than myself could restore me to sanity with respect to alcohol, drugs, cigarettes, anger, food, and family members, certainly I could come to believe that Power could restore me to sanity in the area of negative thinking. It was obvious the 12 Steps would work on *any* addiction as long as I was willing to work them.

Taking the 3rd Step and making the decision to turn my will, my life, and my negative thinking over to the care of God as I understand God is not something I do naturally. Consequently, I often find myself right back in the middle of negative thinking on a grand scale, which in turn motivates me to work the 3rd Step once again, sometimes over and over.

Addictions are like dry ice or hot stoves. Once you touch them, it's hard to let go. The 3rd Step provides the action for letting go and turning it over. Some people write the words "negative thinking" on a piece of paper and place it in a "God box," a place in their homes where they can physically put their addictions, and that's that.

For me, I find it very useful to say the 3rd Step over and over with respect to the particular addiction that is troubling me. If I'm doing a lot of negative thinking, I repeat: "I make the decision to turn my will, my life, and my negative thinking over to the care of God as I understand God," in my own mind over and over again, until the negative thinking goes away. It always does, if I actively work the 3rd Step.

Taking the 4th and 8th Steps and making a list of all the people, places, and things in my life I've hurt by my negative thinking is an integral part of the process of letting go of negative thinking. My negative thinking was a big problem for my parents who, despite the fact they were chronic negative thinkers themselves, suffered at the hands of *my* negative thinking, too.

My father sat with me for hours trying to convince me not to worry about the past or the future, and then he'd go off and worry for hours himself about some problem he had at work. We both fed each other's negative thinking, and as sick people we both need to be understood and forgiven so that the addiction to negative thinking can be released.

Owning my addiction to negative thinking and admitting it

to God, to myself, and to other human beings, Steps 5 and 10, is an excellent way to let go of my negative thinking. When I share my addictions in 12-Step meetings, it helps me to remember where I come from.

Addictions hold on like ticks in August, and total honesty is about the best way to burn them off. There's a saying in the 12-Step programs that we're as sick as our secrets, and I find when I throw those secrets out into the open, they have much less chance to survive. A burden shared is a burden lifted.

Steps 6 and 7 tell us *how* we should go about having our addictions removed. Being *entirely* ready to have the addiction removed and *humbly* asking God to remove it, we must then have the patience to wait until *God* sees fit to remove it. The longer I work the 12 Steps the more power of choice I gain over the various addictions that make up my personality. However, I can't "play" God and determine the exact time and place when a certain addiction will be removed.

Playing God is one of my most self-destructive behaviors. If I continue to acknowledge that *God* removes my addictions and that prayer with humility is the necessary action *I* can take, then *I* can contribute to the partnership and wait for God to do the rest. Then *I* can go ahead and live a healthy, happy, non-addictive way of life to the best of my ability. As soon as I forget to work Steps 6 and 7 with humility, it's strange how fast I slip back into my old addictive ways.

Making amends, Step 9, with respect to negative thinking means not laying negative "trips" onto people and not trying to bring people down. I once had a friend whose mother took one look at me and asked, "Are you part of the problem or part of the solution?" I was surprised how quickly she had my number. I was a walking problem, ignoring every solution that came along. Today I strive to be part of the solution.

I also try not to enable anyone else's negative thinking. It's one thing to listen to someone share his or her negative thinking at a 12-Step meeting, if that person acknowledges his addictive part in it and demonstrates his attempts to let go of it.

It's quite another thing to sit and listen to someone wallow in negative thinking without any admission of his or her part in it. The first example is called sharing our experience, strength, and hope. The second is called *enabling*. The more we enable another person to practice an addiction, the longer they will practice it. I don't have much time today for wallowing in the problem, unless I can see some glimmer of the solution shining through.

The 10th Step: "Continued to take personal inventory and when we were wrong promptly admitted it," is very important to me in order to stay on top of negative thinking. With the help of the 10th Step Mind on an ongoing basis, I observe my thoughts very carefully to make sure I'm not getting bogged down in negative thinking. I've come to realize it's the *first* negative thought that gets me hooked, and so I try to stay away from that first negative thought. Here's an example.

A few months ago my golf partner was canceling out a lot, due to one illness after another. One day he called and said he couldn't play because this time he had some sort of terrible cough, which had come out of nowhere.

When I hung up my mind quickly filled with various negative thoughts. First, I thought his cough must be psychological and he was just malingering because he didn't want to play golf with me, or maybe he just wanted some extra attention. This is negative thinking in the form of paranoia, rejection, and envy.

Then, I thought he must be terribly weak to continue to come down with one illness after another, and because I've been particularly healthy lately this means he is weak and I am strong. This is negative thinking in the form of criticism, comparison, and conceit.

Then, I thought the best way to handle this situation was to find a new golf partner. I'll show him he can't toy with my friendship, I thought. This is negative thinking in the form of anger, resentment, and revenge.

Fortunately for my golfing friendship, my 10th Step Mind was observing this scenario as it unfolded in my mind, and I was able to jam on the brakes before I ran off the cliff with it. I was able to see my addiction to negative thinking was in full swing, and I was able to promptly admit I was wrong.

The pain of many impulsively destroyed friendships in the past motivated me to work the remaining 12 Steps and to let go of the destructive negative thinking about my golf partner. I was able to choose *positive* thoughts instead. I saw my golf partner as a brother rather than an inferior. I felt compassion for him. I released him from any responsibility for my happiness and prayed for his recovery.

These positive thoughts freed me from guilt and gave me a feeling of contentment. Once again the adversity of an addiction forced me to work the 12 Steps, so that my life became a happy, loving, and peaceful experience.

Prayer, meditation, and working with others, Steps 11 and 12, are also very helpful in combating negative thinking. After practicing my thirty-minute morning meditation, my mind usually operates in a positive mode for the rest of the day.

If I slip back into negative thinking, I take a moment to focus on my breathing, or to center myself with a prayer in order to improve my conscious contact with God as I understand God. I also pray for others who suffer from the addiction of negative thinking, and when I find someone who identifies with my addiction to negative thinking, I try to share my experience, strength, and hope for recovery.

Today I have plenty of room in my mind for positive thoughts. Although positive thoughts don't come naturally to me, I find I'm getting better and better at letting them in.

Feelings like empathy, compassion, love, and gratitude, which used to be totally foreign to me, are now becoming a regular part of my daily experience. This improves my relationships with my wife, my family, my friends, and my fellow employees.

Thinking positive thoughts and feeling positive feelings has a positive effect on others. I find I'm not getting physically ill as often as I used to when I was a chronic negative thinker. My productivity at work and my energy for play have improved. In all areas of my life letting go of my addiction to negative thinking has proved beneficial. This has only been possible by working the 12 Steps on negative thinking.

Attending Emotions Anonymous, Emotional Health Anonymous, and 12 Steps for Everybody 12-Step meetings is also quite helpful in dealing with the addiction to negative thinking. In these 12-Step programs we find the fellowship and support of people who understand and care.

We get the chance to remember where we come from with respect to negative thinking and where it would be only too easy for us to return, if we don't continue to work the 12 Steps of recovery. Today I am getting better and better at ignoring the negative and choosing the positive, which is the path to becoming happy, joyous, and free.

Chapter 13

SHOPPING, GAMBLING, & DEBTING

The first time I heard the expression: "When the going gets tough, the tough go shopping," I thought it was hilarious. I also thought it didn't apply to me. Even when I was a kid I hated shopping – the parking problems, the mobs of customers, the pushy sales people. I would do *anything* to avoid shopping, including wearing out-of-date clothes until they were in threads. I didn't even like window-shopping.

Then I remembered twenty-seven years ago when I came into my first 12-Step program jobless, homeless, and $5000 in debt from credit card spending. I had twelve major credit cards. "One was never enough." My plan was to run up those credit cards as high as they would go and then skip to another state, change my name, and get more credit cards.

You can see how brilliantly my mind was operating. Most of the cards had a $3000 limit at that time, so that gave me about $36,000 to play with. The idea that I might get caught never occurred to me.

I didn't get far with the plan. While spending the weekend in another town, I went to pay the motel bill with one of my credit cards. The desk clerk walked away with my card and returned empty-handed wearing a strange look. "The company has asked me to hold your card," he said, brusquely.

"Hold my card! What's the meaning of this?" I replied, indignantly. You know how *irate* we can be. He was immovable. I took out a wad of cash, paid my bill with a flourish, and stalked out of the lobby.

Later, on the train back home, I mulled over what had happened to me. I realized I couldn't go through with my credit card plan. If I wanted to work the 12 Steps and stay sober, I had to be honest, and that meant I had to pay back *all* of the credit card companies. What a shock and what a revelation!

When I arrived home, I gathered up all my credit cards and cut them into pieces. It took me a year to pay off the debts. I remained without a credit card account for two years, until I needed one for check-cashing privileges. Now whenever I use my credit card I always pay back the entire balance every month. I *hate* to pay interest.

I keep records of the cash I spend each day and a monthly budget in order to see where my money goes. I work the 12 Steps on spending, shopping, credit, and debt, because I know how easily I could get out of control again.

My denial regarding money matters goes back a long way. As a teenager I was very frugal and always had a savings account, but as my alcoholism progressed into my twenties I was never able to make ends meet. I got into the habit of spending everything I earned just to *survive*.

My first divorce wiped me out materially, and I lived a hand-to-mouth existence with no savings of any kind. During my second marriage I developed the cavalier attitude that money was to be spent, and I wanted to "live fast, die hard, and make a beautiful corpse." I had never developed a responsible attitude toward money, what it means, or how it should be used.

When my second divorce wiped me out again, I gave up all pretenses at fiscal responsibility. I carried no automobile insurance, no hospitalization insurance, and no life insurance. I had no property, no securities, and no savings. I spent every penny I earned and worked only sporadically when I needed a little extra cash. I wasn't in the red, but I was just *barely* in the black. And there was no provision for an auto accident, a health problem, or death itself. I told myself I was living a "spiritual" life, like a monk with no extra trappings. My denial supported my financial irresponsibility with respect to society, my children, and myself.

By working the 12 Steps on other addictions, my eyes gradually opened to my addiction to irresponsibility in money matters. First, I acknowledged I was breaking the law by not carrying auto insurance, and I might end up without a driver's license if it was discovered I had no liability policy. If I had a bad auto accident, I might even lose the estate income my parents had left for me and my children.

After five years of working the 12 Steps, my mind cleared enough to see that I needed auto insurance, so I bought some. Then a friend of mine was out one night running, tripped on a crack in the sidewalk, and broke her leg in three places. She was in the hospital for six weeks and had a year of physical therapy. The total bill was close to $100,000, but her hospitalization policy covered it all.

I thought about it for a while, went out, and got the same kind of hospitalization policy she had. By working the 12 Steps I was able to let go of my resentment toward insurance companies and to accept the fact that health protection is important.

One thing led to another and I ended up starting a modest individual retirement account. I even purchased some life insurance, so my children wouldn't have to shell out for my burial expenses. Once the "door of awareness" regarding my addiction to debting was opened by working the 12 Steps, I was able to see how irrational and selfish I had been by practicing financial irresponsibility. I was then able to rectify the past, to live wisely in the present, and to prepare unselfishly for the future. I was beginning to become the kind of person I always wanted to be.

Closely related to fiscal irresponsibility has been my lifelong interest in gambling. It all started with the penny ante poker games we had at our family gatherings when I was young. I was a lucky poker player as a kid, and I loved to win. In grade school I started taking bets on college football games and developed a system for getting odds, so I couldn't lose no matter which team won. The school administrators closed me down rather abruptly.

In the medics in the Army, I ran a poker game every night in the medical dispensary where I worked, but I didn't see myself having a problem with gambling because I almost always won. It wasn't until my luck with cards began to change in my mid-twenties that I started to develop a "bottom" on gambling. I was *losing* rather regularly in a seven-card stud game outside of New Orleans, and I wasn't *used* to losing. It hurt.

Then I read about a sure-fire system for winning at black-jack (counting cards) and drove to Las Vegas with my first wife to try it out. The pros had already read the same book and cleaned me out. So much for "systems."

A strange thing happened on that trip to Las Vegas. Late one night while my wife slept in our hotel room upstairs, I found myself in a seven-card stud game winning about $250 and fully aware of the two house shills sitting on each side of me, when I started to feel myself losing control.

I sensed the cards were turning against me, but instead of leaving with my winnings I simply sat there and lost the whole $250, plus $125 *more* of my own. I was sick to my stomach. What *uncanny* force had kept me in that game?

I went upstairs in a state of confusion. I couldn't figure out what was happening. I had heard about compulsive gamblers being compulsive "losers," but I didn't consider myself a compulsive gambler. I'd always been able to quit before. Why had I just sat there and thrown good money after bad? Was I a compulsive *loser*, too?

One night several years later I was playing poker dice with my second wife and having a consistent run of good luck, so I hopped on a plane to the Bahamas and the gambling casino on Paradise Island in Nassau. The exact same thing happened.

This time I was winning about $500, and instead of walking away when my luck turned bad, I just stood there and threw good chips after bad, until I was completely "tapped out."

When I landed in the States I had to call my wife to pick me up, because I didn't have enough money for a bus. The Return of the Big Time Gambler! That was it! No more casino gambling for me!

Some people say that in *recovery* we are doomed to repeat everything we did when we were *practicing* our addiction. With four years of "recovery" in the 12-Step programs, I was doomed to gamble once more in a casino, this time in Atlantic City. I decided to take just $50, no more, no less, and try it out just *one more time* on the crap tables. I told myself if I won $200 I would quit, *or* if I lost the $50 I would quit. I just wanted to see if it was possible for me to quit winners.

I'll never forget that sick feeling of *helplessness* as I stood at the crap table on the boardwalk in Atlantic City, after rolling six straight sevens, $350 ahead, and I was *unable* to walk away. I just stood there with the dice in my hand, completely out of control. I knew the dice were cold. I *knew* I was going to lose. And yet I put all of my chips on the line, rolled the dice, and crapped out. I was only able to quit when I had lost everything!

Now, if that isn't being a compulsive loser, I don't know what is. Who knows what's behind it? Greed? Lust? Guilt? Self-destruction? *Understanding* doesn't help. I have crossed that "invisible line" with respect to gambling. That night in Las Vegas was the beginning of my complete loss of control.

There's nothing worse than that sickening feeling that accompanies the loss of control. You tell yourself you *ought* to stop, but you *can't*. You know you'll have to pay the price later on, but you go ahead and do it anyway. It's as if the whole universe has turned against you and you might as well be dead. So, you might as well "kill" yourself.

It's that sickening feeling, being "sick and tired of being sick and tired," that's been so important to the "bottoms" on my various addictions. It's that sickening feeling which provides the final motivation for working the 12 Steps in order to let go of the addiction. Pain, *once again*, becomes the touchstone of spiritual growth.

Today I work the 12 Steps on my addictions to debt, fiscal irresponsibility, and gambling to the best of my ability. I still purchase a one-dollar lotto ticket now and then. I still play in family poker games, make excursions to the racetrack with friends, and participate in friendly skins games with golf partners. I still pay the interest on my credit card once in a while. And I still operate pretty close to the line when it comes to savings.

But with my Higher Power's help, I no longer allow myself to go "out of control" in any of these areas. I continue on a daily basis to work the 12 Steps on debt, fiscal irresponsibility, and gambling in order to promote a serene and comfortable life.

When it comes to addictive money matters, I must continue to admit I am powerless and my life is unmanageable. I must come to believe on a daily basis that a Power greater than myself can restore me to sanity with respect to addictive money matters, and I must make the daily decision to turn my will, my life, and my addictive money matters over to the care of God as I understand God.

The first three *basic* Steps 1, 2, and 3 enable me to live a fairly sane and constructive existence regarding debt, fiscal irresponsibility, and gambling. The 12-Step programs that address these issues are Debtors Anonymous, Gamblers Anonymous, and The 12 Steps for Everybody. I find their meetings helpful whenever I begin to obsess over addictive money matters.

The combination of *working* the 12 Steps and the supportive *fellowship* of the 12-Step meetings continues to provide the help I need to remain happy, joyous, and free from addiction.

Chapter 14

ENVY & JEALOUSY

The dictionary defines envy as resentment toward someone who has what you want and jealousy as resentment toward someone who threatens what you have. Either way these two "possessions-oriented" defects of character have dealt me my share of pain and suffering. Anyone who has ever longed for someone else's automobile or house or wife knows about envy. And anyone who has ever worried about their girlfriend being with some other man knows about jealousy.

The Bible says we shouldn't covet our neighbor's goods, but that's not easy when our neighbors so often have exactly what we think we want. It doesn't really matter what it is. If you have it, I want it.

As a child I constantly competed with my brother for possessions and attention. I never failed to want what he had. If he got any attention from either of my parents, it drove me nuts. My mother often said to me, "You're never satisfied!" And she was right. It didn't matter what she did for me or how much, I was never satisfied.

I believe *greed* is closely allied with envy, and the two can augment each other. I once had a psychoanalyst who told me I had an excessive amount of envy. Little did either of us realize I was *addicted* to it.

"Jealousy," resenting those who threaten what I already have, goes way back to the day my baby brother came into the house and usurped my "throne." My world crumbled, and I never recovered from that unscrupulous invasion of my territory. All you have to do today is smile too much at my wife or get some attention from the boss and I'm jealous.

If you admire my house or compliment my car, I begin to suspect you and start to keep my distance. *Distrust* is an addiction, which often accompanies my jealousy. I become mentally violent toward people of whom I am jealous. I hate handsome men who pass within view of my wife. I loathe fellow workers who sit in my boss's office having friendly conversations. When my kids tell me about some teacher or parent they admire, I seethe with jealousy.

Anger is definitely a co-addiction with jealousy for me. The two feed on each other. Besides greed, distrust, and anger what other *payoffs* are there for envy and jealousy? When I indulge in *envy*, I am "rewarded" by the resentment I can entertain toward the person who has what I want. Being envious of other people's jobs, looks, or money enables me to wallow in self-pity.

I can hate the person I envy and feel sorry for myself at the same time. I can also indulge in the vicarious thrill of imagining what it would be like if I had what they have. *Fantasizing* having what other people have allows me to sit around *slothfully* doing nothing to actually get what I want. The drama and adrenaline generated from the resentment, anger, self-pity, and fantasy sends me on an emotional jag. Then I can top the whole thing off with a nice, big, heaping portion of *guilt*.

Jealousy can generate the same payoffs as envy, plus more. With jealousy you usually have a more distinct adversary to project your bad feelings onto, someone who threatens to take away what you already have. The indignation which arises can be much more righteous. And for me jealousy just naturally leads to paranoid suspicion over what that someone is up to. I often suspect they have it in their minds to harm me, which triggers off a whole mental scenario as to how I'm going to protect myself.

I reached my bottom on envy and jealousy during the tumultuous relationship with my second ex-wife. While we were married, psychoanalysis brought me in touch with the strange fact that I not only *envied* what my second wife had, I wanted to *be* her. I had such a low opinion of myself that I didn't even want to be *me*. This is the ultimate insanity to which an addiction to envy can be carried. I was also insanely jealous of everyone and everything with which my ex-wife came into contact.

A year after we were divorced, I went into a suicidal anxiety depression due mainly to envy and jealousy. I envied the successful way her life was going, and I was jealous of the things in her life that kept her from taking me back.

For seven excruciatingly painful months my envy and jealousy kept me more wrapped up in who my ex-wife was than who I was. It was impossible for me to live my own life, I was so fixated on *her*. I knew envy and jealousy were eating me alive but "awareness" alone was not enough to enable me to let go of this "codependent" addiction.

How could I learn to be happy with who I was, instead of craving to be someone else? In my case it was necessary for me to work the 12 Steps on my addiction to envy and jealousy in order to let go of them. I had to be willing to admit I was powerless over envy and jealousy and that my life had become unmanageable. I had to come to believe that a Power greater than myself could restore me to sanity and take away my envy and jealousy.

I had to make the decision to turn my will, my life, and my envy and jealousy over to the care of God as I understood God. If I didn't take these first three Steps on envy and jealousy, I knew my addiction would make it impossible for me to live my own life and to be happy with who I am.

Steps 4 through 12 were also paramount to my liberation from these particular addictions. I wrote every day about my envy and jealousy regarding the people, places, and things in my past, and I shared my writings with others.

I became entirely ready to have God remove these addictive defects of character, and I humbly asked God to do so. I made it a point to pray for anyone for whom I felt envy and jealousy, and I monitored my feelings with my 10th Step Mind, promptly cutting myself short whenever I felt the first pang of envy or jealousy toward anyone.

It was a long slow process letting go of envy and jealousy, and I know today I am not entirely home free. A few months ago I had an experience, which proved this true. One day at work I began to notice one of the young women in my office was not saying hello to me. Even though I smiled and said hello to her, she rarely returned the courtesy. I began to obsess over it and developed a big resentment.

When she ignored my greeting, I took it as a personal rejection. My feelings were hurt. Sometimes on the weekends I would think about how *cruel* she was, not saying hello to me, and I would wish horrible things would happen to her. My obsession over this slight grew and grew. I felt tremendous rage when she paid attention to others and ignored me.

I fantasized situations where I could get revenge. Perhaps I'd win a million dollars in the lottery and *then* she would want to pay attention to me! I'd throw a big party and invite everybody in the office but her. *Then* she'd see what a mean person she had been to me and she'd experience the same pain of rejection I suffered at her hands.

Working the 10th and 11th Steps on my predicament, I struggled to identify the addictive defects of character, which might be involved. It seemed to be resentment and over-sensitivity to rejection, and so I worked the remaining 12 Steps like a beaver in order to let go of my discomfort and hurt feelings.

For several weeks I admitted I was powerless over my resentment and over-sensitivity regarding this woman and that my life had become unmanageable. I shared my resentment and over-sensitivity at meetings, admitted that I was wrong, became entirely ready to have God remove these defects, and humbly asked God to remove these shortcomings.

I worked the 12 Steps on resentment and over-sensitivity to the best of my ability, but it didn't seem to be doing any good. Every time she didn't say hello I was thrown back into the depths of despair. My happiness and well-being became *directly* proportional to whether or not this woman at work said hello to me. Does this qualify for insanity?

Returning to the 10th and 11th Steps in order to gain some clue as to what I was doing wrong, I noticed that a few other women at work ignored me also, but it didn't seem to *bother* me at all. The difference between them and this particular woman was that she was young, beautiful, and talented. She had a great future. She was what I considered a "successful" human being.

I was finally able to get in touch with the fact that I had a great deal of *envy* of her. The addiction, which had remained hidden *beneath* resentment and over-sensitivity, was envy! I wanted what she had: youth, good looks, talent, and success, but I hadn't been able to admit it to myself.

Once I identified the *primary* addiction I was able to work the 12 Steps on it, and the whole thing went away. From then on I felt comfortable at work whether or not the young woman said hello.

Envy is an addiction that tells me I don't have enough. I don't have enough youth, enough health, enough looks, enough money, enough success, enough love. The "hole" inside me cries out for *more*, and when I look around I see people who have what I think can fill that hole, and I envy them.

Working the 11th Step I came to realize that the only thing that could fill that hole and take away my envy was the Higher Power I came in contact with when I worked the 11th Step. Having the Higher Power was *enough*. And for those brief moments when I experienced that conscious contact with my

Higher Power, I felt like I was enough, too. Then and only then, I envied no one.

My life today is so much better when I work the 12 Steps on envy and jealousy. No longer do I have to suffer the painful craving for something someone else has. My relationships with my wife, my fellow workers, and even complete strangers are much more loving and enjoyable, when I don't need to indulge in envy and jealousy. I can appreciate what I have today and not fear losing it. I can enjoy life on life's terms without wishing I was somebody else.

As long as I realize I have only a daily reprieve from envy and jealousy, based on my spiritual condition and the 12 Steps that maintain it, the freedom and joy of being "enough" follows me everywhere.

The 12-Step meetings which apply to envy and jealousy are Emotions Anonymous, Emotional Health Anonymous, and The 12 Steps for Everybody. If you don't have any of these programs in the area where you live, you can telephone the nearest large city, or go on the Internet, to obtain information about starting your own group.

Even if you can't attend 12-Step meetings, the 12 Steps will work on your addictions if you work them.

Chapter 15

SHAME & GUILT

Guilt has been a way of life for me in a world where I felt everybody else was right, and I was wrong. I just naturally thought because you were *you* and I was *me*, I had a good reason to feel guilty. Some people say "shame" is generalized bad feelings about oneself, while "guilt" has a legitimate origin for the bad feeling. I've been addicted to shame and guilt for so long that whatever you call it, I've had enough to last me a lifetime.

Growing up in a dysfunctional family, we all practiced shame and guilt on a regular basis. It was modeled by everyone around me. As long as we worked hard, sacrificed a lot, and suffered enough, we didn't have to feel guilty, but as soon as things started going smoothly the guilt came down on our heads like an avalanche.

We always expected the *worst* when things went well, because that's what we thought we deserved – the worst. Here are some of the things, which cause me to indulge in guilt:

– Having fun or enjoying myself.
– Being loved or admired.
– Receiving compliments or gifts.
– Being rewarded or promoted.
– Seeing other people in pain or trouble.
– Standing up for myself.
– Trying to better myself.
– Expressing emotions like anger, fear, or love.
– Saying what's really on my mind.
– Being myself.

I can feel guilty about anything, if I'm in the mood to practice guilt. I believe I have a genetic and hormonal predisposition toward guilt. Once I discovered it could provide the kind of fix I needed to escape other more painful thoughts and feelings, I became *habituated* to guilt. The *payoffs* became a necessary part of my existence.

By working Steps 4, 5, and 10 on guilt, I discovered that basically I believe I am a *bad* person. Deep down inside I feel that I'm rotten to the core, and I don't deserve to live, much less have anything *good* happen to me.

Even though I know my mother loved me, I also know that she abused me physically, mentally, emotionally, and sexually. Through the years I accepted this abuse as the punishment due me for being a bad person.

Whenever anything good happens to me today, I feel guilty in order to avoid my mother's hatred, anger, abuse, and punishment. It doesn't matter that my mother has been dead for forty-four years. The hatred, anger, abuse, and punishment are *alive* in me today, and so one of the biggest payoffs of addictive guilt for me is that it saves me from having to feel self-hatred, self-anger (depression), self-abuse, and self-punishment.

I also learned by working Steps 4, 5, and 10 that I feel I am to blame for most of the bad things that happen around me. When I was a kid and caddied for my father, every time he hit a bad golf shot I felt guilty. (He would always glare at me, as though it was my fault.)

My self-worth was determined by what kind of golf shot my father made, and I felt I deserved to be punished if he made a bad shot. To this day whenever I see other people in any kind of pain or trouble, I always feel guilty because it protects me from intense feelings of self-blame and self-punishment.

Any form of self-assertion or manifestation of my own identity brings on guilt for me. As a child I perceived self-assertion as a direct threat to my parents, who gave me hatred, anger, abuse, and punishment in return for my self-assertion. I could be a good boy, an outstanding boy, if I did what *they* wanted, but if I did what I wanted I was in danger of attack and the withdrawal of love.

Standing up for myself, expressing my emotions, and saying what is really on my mind are situations that bring me tremendous guilt. The very act of being myself is a "crime" in my own mind, for which I need guilt to protect myself from fear of attack and the withdrawal of love.

Like all of my other emotional addictions, the last resort for letting go of guilt has been the 12 Steps, but I didn't begin to work them on guilt until I had been in my first 12-Step program for over seven years. One day I finally reached my bottom on guilt. I had spent an enjoyable day with a friend and a wonderful evening with my wife, and the next morning I woke up with a crippling backache.

I had been troubled with this disabling back pain since I was twelve, whenever I went on vacation or did anything I really enjoyed doing. It had defied medical and psychiatric treatment. I knew exactly where it came from. I felt guilty about the fun I'd had the day before, and the backache was my own form of self-punishment.

I resolved then and there that I had finally had enough guilt. I was sick and tired of being sick and tired of feeling guilty, and I committed myself to working the 12 Steps in order to kick my guilt habit.

I admitted I was powerless over my addiction to guilt and my life had become unmanageable. I came to believe a Power greater than myself could restore me to sanity and take away my chronic guilt. I made a decision to turn my will, my life, and my guilt over to the care of God as I understood God.

For the past twenty years I have worked the 12 Steps on guilt, and I have enjoyed much relief from this crippling addiction. Surrendering, believing, deciding, searching, admitting, becoming ready, humbly asking, listing, making amends, inventorying, meditating, and working with others have all played an important role in my struggle to let go of guilt.

What does it mean when a particular addiction resists the onslaught of the 12 Steps? Guilt is not the first tenacious addiction I've experienced. My addiction to alcohol lasted twenty-seven years for me. Drugs hung on for twelve. Even with the help of the 12 Steps and the attainment of sobriety from alcohol, drugs, and cigarettes, it took me two more years to let go of anger, four more years for family members, five more years for anxiety and depression, and eight more years for codependence.

In my attempts to let go of addictive guilt, I have discovered that guilt falls into that category of *intangible* addictions, which are most basic to my personality and consequently the most difficult for me to release. I hold onto guilt because it is "me." And yet the tenacity of guilt turns out to be a blessing in disguise, because in my struggle with it I have learned more of what I need to learn about my own spiritual path of recovery.

Working Steps 2, 3, 4, 6, 7, 10, and 11, I have come to realize that I don't have to indulge in guilt just because I sometimes experience human feelings like lust, envy, or resentment. I don't have to practice guilt just because I'm not perfect. I don't even need to wallow in guilt when I do something wrong.

Feeling guilty doesn't *change* anything. It doesn't right the wrong. It doesn't cause me to change. It only gets me “off the hook,” so I can turn around and do the same thing all over again. No, indulging in guilt doesn't rectify or absolve wrongful acts for a guilt junkie like me. It only tends to perpetuate them. The only way I can change is by working the 12 Steps and turning my will and my life over to a Power greater than myself.

Even though I am not entirely free of guilt today, my bouts with it are shorter, fewer, and farther between. This is what the 12-Step fellowship saying: "Keep coming back!" really means. We might not be able to let go of an addiction immediately or entirely. It could take time, a lot of time. The addiction might seem to be gone entirely, and then return in one fell swoop. That's when we need to work the 12 Steps on it even more rigorously than before. Perseverance is the key when it comes to working the 12 Steps.

How do I recognize when I am indulging in addictive guilt? By using the 10th Step Mind on a continuous basis. Whenever I experience *any* negative emotion for longer than five minutes, I know I am wrong and I promptly admit it.

Once I can acknowledge it's a mistake for me to feel guilty, I can usually decide *not* to indulge in any more guilt for that day. I decide I've had *enough*. I repeat to myself the first three Steps. I write about it and share the writing with others on the telephone and at meetings. I pray and meditate. I work with others who suffer an addiction to guilt similar to mine. Sharing my experience, strength, and hope regarding guilt puts "money" in my "emotional sobriety bank." That way I don't have to suffer an emotional "binge" for one more day.

I only have a daily reprieve from guilt, contingent upon the maintenance of my spiritual condition. In no time at all I can start "binging" on guilt again without the daily help of the 12 Steps.

Guilt is closely allied with judgmentalism, criticism, and condemnation. I'm a person who's addicted to all three. One of my favorite pastimes is judging, criticizing, and condemning myself and others. And it's impossible for guilt to exist without judgment, criticism, and condemnation.

Since I know I'll never be entirely free of judgment, criticism, and condemnation, it's all the more important for me to work those Steps which contain "acceptance" and "forgiveness" – Steps 1 through 5, 8, 9, and 11. Freedom from guilt lies in acceptance and forgiveness of myself and others. Working these particular Steps heightens my practice of acceptance and forgiveness and lowers my practice of guilt.

The 12-Step groups applicable to working the 12 Steps on guilt are Emotions Anonymous, Emotional Health Anonymous, and The 12 Steps for Everybody. Starting a 12-Step meeting to address *your* addictions and to *work* with others with the same addictions will open up a new way of life for you, a way of life that brings peace, joy, and contentment.

Chapter 16

OBSESSION & COMPULSION

When I went into the mental institution at age seventeen, they diagnosed me as "psychoneurotic with obsessive-compulsive tendencies." I thought that was kind of wimpy at the time. Considering my delusions of grandeur and feelings of persecution, I figured I deserved at least "paranoid schizophrenic," but I found out later they didn't want to ruin my future career chances with such a serious psychiatric history.

Little did I realize that the obsessive-compulsive tendencies alone were enough to ruin my life. I showed signs of obsessive-compulsive behavior from an early age. "Step on a crack and break your mother's back!" was a childhood phrase we recited as we skipped along the sidewalks, making sure we stepped on all the seams which separated each square of cement.

I felt terribly guilty, because I didn't really want to break my mother's back, so most of the time I made sure *not* to step on the cracks. I reversed the *compulsion*. That way I thought I was being kind to my mother. When I got angry at her, I practiced the compulsion by stepping *on* the sidewalk cracks. It gave me a gratifying sense of power and control over whether or not my mother suffered.

Acting out my addiction to compulsion on the sidewalks of the neighborhood where I grew up provided an immediate *payoff* for me as a child. It gave me the feeling I had some power and control over my universe.

From six to twelve I had a lot of dental work done. Every year there was the agonizing trip to the dentist in which three or more new cavities were discovered. Then there were the interminable dental appointments, spaced three weeks apart, during which I returned over and over again for the painful drilling and filling.

It was a nightmare not so much because of the pain, but because during those periods between the appointments I would be *obsessed* almost constantly with worry over the future pain. The addictive obsession was worse than the thing I was obsessed over. But if it hadn't been the dental appointments, I would have found *something else* to satisfy my craving for obsession.

Obsession and compulsion are fed by anxiety, depression, envy, negative thinking, resentment, and any other idea, desire, or emotion that can stimulate enough mental, emotional, or physical energy to trigger them. Sugar triggers my compulsion to overeat. Photos of nude women trigger my obsession with sex. Just about anything can stimulate obsessive behavior or compulsive action on my part.

As a youngster I greatly feared going to bed at night. I hated turning out the light and lying in the darkness – isolated, separate, and alone. My anxiety at bedtime set off a number of compulsive acts. Every night I had to look in the closet, check under the bed, pick all the lint off the rug, touch the corner of my desk, touch the four bedposts, and kneel down to say my prayers before I switched off the light and crawled into bed.

I had to perform all of these acts before I could get to sleep. If I forgot even *one* of them I would have to get up, turn on the light, and go through the whole compulsive ritual again until I got it right. This was one of the ways I fed my addiction to compulsion.

Obsession and compulsion are addictions in their own right, regardless of the idea, desire, or emotion, which stimulates them. Because they are so closely intertwined with anxiety, depression, envy, negative thinking, and resentment, the denial systems of obsession and compulsion are almost impossible to break.

Take the Family Members' addiction of obsessing over the well-being of a child. Since we're the parent and the child is *our* child, we're convinced we have a perfect right, even a *duty*, to obsess over the child all day long. If the child is in some kind of trouble or difficulty, all the more reason to be obsessed.

Try to convince an obsession junkie to forget the child, work the 12 Steps, and live his or her own life, and you're in for trouble. Obsessions hold on like leeches. They don't let go until we become so pitifully and incomprehensibly demoralized we're willing to go to any lengths to give them up.

The world of obsession is a world of memory, daydream, and fantasy. We obsess over something, which already happened, something we wish was happening now, or something we wish or fear will happen in the future. Most of my life has been spent in one of these three forms of obsession. In grade school the teachers threw erasers at me in class to wake me out of daydreams, but you don't stop an obsession addict with force.

In college my tendency to fantasize destroyed my concentration and my grades. A writing career was completely ruined by my mind's addiction to thinking about anything other than the subject in front of me. Throughout it all I was not the least bit aware I was addicted to obsession. I thought I merely suffered from a lack of "will power."

Indulging in obsession provides some rather comprehensive payoffs. The first is that obsession is the ideal vehicle for practicing other intangible addictions like anger, resentment, fear, envy, and guilt. Obsession is a mental process in which the mind plays an idea, desire, or emotion over and over again like a videotape in the brain. It doesn't matter how often we play the obsession tape. It keeps playing over and over until we tire of it and go on to another tape (obsession), or until we become distracted and stop obsessing for the moment.

Engaging in obsession allows us to indulge in other addictions without taking action. Obsession is the lazy man's way of accomplishing things. One of my chronic addictions is the idea or fantasy of becoming rich and famous. It's an obsession I've entertained since I was six years old, but for which I've taken no real positive action. All my life I've wanted to be rich and famous. I've dreamed about it. I've fantasized about it. But I've never actually done anything to *actualize* the obsession. Why? Because it's much easier to *obsess* over something than it is to *do* it.

Another payoff for practicing obsession is escape. Obsession has the capacity to mask painful ideas and emotions like fear, inadequacy, and boredom. All I have to do is turn on my obsession machine – my mind – and I'm immediately in the middle of a memory, daydream, or fantasy which lifts me out of the painful feelings of fear, inadequacy, or boredom.

Some people confuse fantasy/obsession with imagination. I believe it's a question of degree. A little imagination comes in handy sometimes, but a lot of imagination turns into obsession, which has the power to remove me from reality and to thereby ruin my life. In the long run I've discovered it's much better to face the painful ideas and emotions of reality than to escape them with obsession.

Obsession is a way of trying to gain *control* of reality. It's an attempt to actually *change what is* with our minds. We think if we obsess over something long enough and hard enough it will come to pass the way we want it. The tape loop keeps repeating itself in the hope that the obsession will become actualized.

In my case I have sat for hours, days, months, and even years obsessing over some job or woman, while my *real life* went ignored and unattended. The frustration that built up during these obsessions was tremendous. I was robbing myself of a real life by obsessing over a life that wasn't mine. Even being sick and tired of being sick and tired was not enough to reach a bottom.

My bottom finally came with the obsession I developed over my second ex-wife. It lasted the first nine years of my sobriety and spanned the continent: six geographic moves, seven jobs, and eight romantic relationships.

My obsession over my second ex-wife was based on the transference of unresolved mental and emotional conflicts centering on my long-deceased mother, and it entailed all of the addictive defects of character I had operating around that dynamic: fear (of abandonment, separation, rejection, loneliness, insecurity), paranoia (alienation from others, competitiveness, adversarial relationships, distrust), resentment (envy of others, unfulfilled lust, anger at injustice), and lack of identity (low or no self-esteem, vicarious living, people-pleasing).

One does not have to understand the psychodynamics of an obsession to work the 12 Steps on it and to begin to let go of it. The psychic pain of the fear, paranoia, resentment, and lack of identity was enough to force me to work the Steps on the ex-wife obsession for the nine years over which it unfolded without understanding much about it at all.

I admitted I was powerless over my obsession regarding my second ex-wife and my life had become unmanageable. I came to believe a Power greater than myself could restore me to sanity and take away my obsession over my second ex-wife. And I made the decision to turn my will, my life, and my obsession regarding my second ex-wife over to the care of God, as I understood God.

I received some relief from the obsession from the very beginning, and there were times when I thought it had gone away completely, but then it would return much to my dismay and I would be right back in the middle of it again. By working Steps 4, 5, 10, 11, and 12, I was able to see that the obsession was made up of a *cluster* of smaller addictive pieces: lust, pride, envy, and resentment.

I worked the 12 Steps on each of these *pieces* of the obsession and sometimes it went away. I wrote booklets of inventory on the obsession and shared it with others. I continued to take inventory and when I found myself obsessing over my second ex-wife, I promptly admitted I was wrong to do so and attempted to stop it.

I prayed and meditated on a daily basis in order to stay in touch with a Power greater than myself, reaching out for knowledge of God's will for me and the power to carry that out. I was on the telephone every day with others who suffered from addictive obsession, and I shared my experience, strength, and hope with them so we could mutually recover from our obsessions.

Some confusion arose from time to time when I would let go of one of the pieces of the cluster and the obsession seemed to be gone, and then it *returned* again. This caused some disappointment at first, but I simply continued to work the 12 Steps on the whole obsession and success eventually occurred.

By working the 12 Steps on lust I lost my sexual attraction for my second ex-wife and thought I was finished with the obsession once and for all. When it returned I had to work the 12 Steps again in order to discover that pride and my damaged ego at her not taking me back was now refueling the obsession and causing me to dwell on her once again. When I let go of pride, envy raised its ugly head. I *envied* my second ex-wife's financial, occupational, and social achievements, and I *resented* her tremendous success in an area of the business world in which I was severely lacking.

I had to work the 12 Steps separately on envy and resentment, because as long as there was a single addictive defect of character to feed it, the *overall* obsession remained. When I was able by the use of the 12 Steps to let go of envy and resentment, the obsession went away. I was free at last from a nine-year obsession.

One final example of the power of the 12 Steps, especially the 11th Step in letting go of addictive obsessions, is seen in an experience I once had with a dual obsession. One morning seventeen years ago, as I left the house for work, I began to obsess over fear of economic insecurity and abandonment. I started to worry that I didn't have enough money to live, and it seemed that everyone in my life was rejecting me.

These two obsessive thoughts wrestled with each other in my mind as I drove my car to work. Back and forth I vacillated between fear of financial destitution and feelings of rejection, when suddenly while walking from the parking lot to the office I discovered that if I focused my attention on my *breathing* the obsessions went away. Fear of economic insecurity and the feeling of rejection left me when I gave my attention to my breathing.

I had discovered yet another method of practicing the 11th Step, and I could do it while I was driving my car, walking on the sidewalk, or sitting at my desk at work. All I had to do was focus on my breathing and I was free of obsession, free to be in the "here and now" without the excess baggage of obsessive thoughts and feelings.

The benefits of an obsession- and compulsion-free existence are tremendous. Having your thoughts and feelings connected to what's going on around you in the *reality of the moment* is a reward that turns life into a whole new experience. Being able to decide what you *do* and *don't* want to think about and do is a blessing, which enriches every moment in the day. Giving your complete attention to your loved ones makes interpersonal relationships a delight.

Without the chains of obsession and compulsion to distract us and hold us down, we can stay and live in the moment. It's a much better life when we are fully present for it. It's easy to get discouraged with the slowness of recovery from addictions like obsession and compulsion. I know I'll never be fully recovered from them, but I am enjoying the experience of *progress* toward freedom from obsession and compulsion.

Today I spend less and less time in obsession and compulsion and more and more time in the present. *Patience* with the process of recovery is what counts when it comes to letting go of these two addictions. *Persistence* along the path of recovery from obsession and compulsion is seen in regular attendance at 12-Step meetings of Emotions Anonymous, Emotional Health Anonymous, and The 12 Steps for Everybody.

Someone once asked, "If I feel better, why should I continue to go to the meetings?" At the meetings we can practice all of the 12 Steps on an ongoing basis. We can't keep it (freedom from addiction), unless we give it away.

Nor can we keep it if we take it for granted. As soon as we begin to take freedom from an addiction for granted, it will rise up and grab us around the throat again. This is especially true of obsession and compulsion.

Chapter 17

WORK

It has been said that "all work and no play makes Jack a dull boy." Not true for me. When I enter the work mode, I become an anxiety-ridden, tyrannical, homicidal maniac. The reason is that all my life "work," otherwise known as occupation, profession, or career, has been the major factor in my *identity*. Without my work I am nothing.

You can take away my romance, my children, my creature comforts, even my health, but don't take away my *work*. How did this thing called work grow into such an addiction for me?

When I was a kid looking around innocently for something to become addicted to, my parents told me I could be anything I wanted to be when I grew up, even President of the United States. I immediately took this to mean:

A) The most important task in my life is to choose the proper career.
B) The best career to choose is the one that will bring me the most money, property, and prestige.
C) If I don't become somebody *important*, I might as well be *dead*.

Probably most kids don't react the way I did to that saying about becoming President; but I bet for little girls it's something like, "You can be anything you want to be when you grow up, even Miss America." We're all too familiar with the socioeconomic ideals we're fed as children. Little girls are supposed to be pretty and nice, so they can get a good husband. Little boys are supposed to be tough and smart, so they can make a lot of money.

Maybe it all works out well for the "average" person, but

for one such as I, whose addictive brain takes *molehills* and turns them into *mountains* at the blink of an eye, telling me I can become President is the same thing as telling me if I *don't* become President, I'm totally worthless.

I equate what I *am* occupationally with what I *am* as a human being. My identity, my very being as an individual, is equivalent to the profession I'm supposed to choose and pursue until I'm successful at it. And success, of course, is measured in terms of fame and fortune. My self-worth is equal to my worth in the market place. This addictive and malevolent idea started taking its toll on me from the start.

At ten years of age, I lay awake nights trying to decide whether I should be a surgeon or a stockbroker. I tossed and turned and considered the alternatives between law, management, and sales. Was science or research the proper route? It was a quandary I couldn't solve, because any *one* choice might be the *wrong* one! And then what would I do? I would have to kill myself.

When I was twelve, I told my parents I either wanted to be a millionaire or a bum. The psychological pressure of trying to choose the *right* profession was already getting to me. I thought perhaps I could escape it by going to the other extreme and becoming a hobo.

After my nervous breakdown at seventeen, the question of what to become occupationally became an unsolvable riddle that I pursued like the Greeks sought the unicorn, thoroughly convinced that once I found the answer, all my problems would be solved. To this day I have *yet* to discover what I *should* become occupationally. Instead, by working the 12 Steps on my addiction to occupational identity and work, I have discovered that it doesn't really *matter* what I do in the way of work, as long as I live a good life.

The 12 Steps have taught me that my self-worth as an individual is *not* measured in terms of money, property, and prestige. My self-worth is measured in terms of joy, peace of mind, and my capacity to love. What a tremendous relief *that* is!

Work for me hasn't only been an addictive attempt at occupational identity. It has also been a means of validating myself through the vigorous activity of productive labor itself. From a very early age I used the amount of work I did over time to measure my self-worth. I worked long hours into the night on my school homework, intensely proud of the vast quantities of math problems, reading, and writing exercises I turned out.

The amount of work I turned out became a *payoff* for my self-esteem. If I didn't meet my personal homework standards and quotas, I felt guilty and unworthy. Every night in grade school, junior high, and high school, I studied at least five or six hours, often longer. I only allowed myself to relax a little on the weekends, and I kept up this grueling schedule until I became a weekend alcoholic at the age of fifteen.

Only then did my capacity for homework start to fail and my grades began to slip. The pace was wearing me down. The stress was almost unbearable. My addiction to work performance was pushing me toward a "bottom."

Another payoff I found in work was escape. I used work to escape from boredom, obsession, and paranoia. Over the past fifty-six work years I have held *fifty* different jobs, professions, and careers, many of them quite boring, because there was not enough actual work involved to provide the challenge I needed to keep me entertained and worthy.

My usual modus operandi at home is to eat dinner, talk on the phone, play Internet chess, and fold my laundry all at the same time. I am one who is very easily bored, and because boredom is extremely painful for me emotionally, I've always required my environment to provide *constant* entertainment.

When I'm bored I feel abandoned, rejected, guilty, anxious, and depressed. Work, if it's entertaining enough, takes me away from these painful feelings. The job has to keep me busy and active. If it doesn't, it has to provide the opportunity to create "busy work," work that doesn't really *need* to be done, but you can do it anyway.

As long as I can convince myself that there's some *merit* to the busy work, I can escape the feelings of abandonment, rejection, guilt, anxiety, and depression. When the occupation doesn't keep me busy enough or entertained enough, I have to quit and go on to another position. In the past I've also depended upon work to escape from obsession. When my mind is not active, it just naturally gravitates toward obsession: remembering, daydreaming, and fantasizing. Often the content of my obsessions is negative and therefore painful.

If the work I'm doing is mentally *active* enough, my mind remains free from painful obsession. If it's not, I usually suffer from obsession. The same is true of paranoia. In fact, I reached my bottom on my addiction to work at a job that had so little work to do that I suffered from paranoia almost constantly.

Paranoia is defined as "delusions of grandeur and/or feelings of persecution." At this particular job there was no opportunity for busy work, and the supervisors were constantly watching to make sure you didn't read or write things that were non-job-related. I read the policy and procedures manual over and over again, day in and day out, until I wanted to hang myself in the men's room.

On this particular job I could see the *direct* relationship between the times when I had work to do and was paranoia-free, compared to the times when I had no work to do and was overwhelmed with paranoia. In this case my paranoia took the form of thinking my fellow employees hated me and were out to get me, even though there was no *real* basis for this belief. I could see I was using work as an escape, that I was indeed *addicted* to work, and that I needed to start practicing the 12 Steps on work if I was ever to hold a job on a continuous and sustained basis.

I saw I was never going to find a job where there were not some lapses in work activity. Over the years I had been hopping from job to job in a desperate and vain attempt to find the impossible, a job that would keep me busy and entertained all the time, so that I wouldn't be bored, obsessed, or paranoid.

Working the 12 Steps on addictive work, especially Steps 4, 5, and 10, I was able to get a very clear picture of the way I had used work addictively over the years for identity, validation, and *escape* from painful emotions.

By working Step 1, I saw how my life had become unmanageable in other ways besides job-hopping. Being a workaholic had affected my relations with others, my health, and my family. Needing work to fill that gaping hole in my gut, I had stolen time from my friends, my relations, and myself and had given it to the god of work. Was I sick and tired of being sick and tired of addictive work? It seemed I had finally reached that bottom.

About nineteen years ago I came to believe a Power greater than myself could restore me to sanity and take away my need to work addictively. No longer was I willing to *work* myself into such a physically run-down state that I caught one flu virus after another throughout the winter. No more did I want to *work* myself into a frenzy every afternoon, until I got a migraine headache or an attack of spastic colon and had to go home and lie down to get rid of the pain. I had *abused* work and now obviously it was abusing me.

Was beating myself up with work in this fashion insane? I finally came to believe it was. In order to be able to give up the insanity of addictive work, I knew Step 3 would be critical. I had to make the decision to turn my will, my life, and my addiction to work over to the care of God as I understood God. If I had the power to cure my insanity regarding work I would readily do it.

If the knowledge obtained from some book or therapist was sufficient, I would most certainly have used it. However, I had already learned from experience that when it comes to addiction, no *human* power or knowledge is sufficient. Relief from my addictions has depended over and over again on a Power much greater than myself or anyone else.

With Step 3, I committed myself, my will, and my life completely to that Power which can restore me to sanity in the area of work, and that power is God. Inventory, sharing, and becoming entirely *ready* to have my addiction to work removed are the business of Steps 4, 5, and 6.

Humbly asking that Power greater than myself to remove my addiction to work is Step 7, a Step that has demanded a lot of patience on my part over the years. Just because I think I'm entirely ready to have an addiction removed doesn't necessarily mean that humbly asking the Higher Power to remove it is going to work right away.

Sometimes the removal is *slow* and sometimes it is *painful*. There are times when I even get quite angry with my Higher Power, because I don't think that the addiction is being removed fast enough. Later I see that there is usually a purpose for the slow removal of a particular defect of character, and that purpose often has something to do with my needing to *learn* something more from the addiction before I am *really* ready to let go of it.

Although I have been able to let go of some of my addictive work behavior with the help of the 12 Steps, there is still a lot of room for recovery. One of the Step 9 amends I have made to *myself* is a fifteen-minute break in the morning and a fifteen-minute break in the afternoon, wherever I'm employed. For a long time I was unable to take even a one-minute break for fear of angering the boss and losing my job. Now I'm able to take two fifteen-minute breaks without feeling too much anxiety or guilt.

Sometimes I cut the break short, or I don't take it at all, because I don't feel I deserve it. That old addiction to work as a means of self-worth gets in the way. Sometimes I find myself working so hard I get a headache, or I get so tired I'm ready to drop. Then I know I'm not practicing the principles of the 12 Steps on my work addiction, and I make a renewed effort to do the Steps more thoroughly. One day at a time I get better, if I persist with the 12 Steps.

Throughout the history of the 12-Step programs, the slogans have been a very useful supplement to the 12 Steps. "One Day at a Time" is very helpful with respect to tangible addictions, because it encourages us to stay in the moment without demanding too much of ourselves over an impossible period of time.

"Live and Let live" is particularly useful for the addictions to family members and codependence, because it reinforces the reality of letting other people live their own lives exclusive of what we think is best for them.

"Let Go and Let God" is the 3rd Step slogan, constantly reminding us that "I can't, God can, and I think I'll let God." For my addiction to work, my slogan of choice is "Easy Does It." Easy Does It is not easy for me. I've always been a power-driver and a speed freak, so telling me I have to take it easy is like chaining me to a tree. It goes against my nature to “take it easy.”

I feel like I'm committing a crime and deserve to be dipped in hot hog fat, when I take it easy. But Easy Does It has become a necessity for me today in order to preserve my sanity. My addiction to work has brought me to the point where if I don't take it easy, I'm simply condemning myself to more physical, mental, emotional, and spiritual grief.

Easy Does It for me means the work will get done eventually, so why kill myself doing it? What's the big rush? It'll be there tomorrow. What more do I gain from doing it today? Of course, there are others who are not only *not* addicted to work; they're addicted to *non-work*, the opposite extreme. These people are procrastinators. Their motto is: "Why do today what you can put off until tomorrow?"

For these people the necessary slogan reads: "Easy Does It, But Do It!" But not so for me. I have to use the 12 Steps to put on the brakes. Otherwise, I run off the road of serenity and end up in a ditch of work frenzy, which destroys me.

Recently I discovered a new way of using the 11th Step on an ongoing basis on my addiction to work. You merely pick the personification of any Higher Power you want – Jesus, Moses, Mohammed, Buddha, any of the saints or spiritual leaders in history – and you imagine that Personification is with you throughout the day.

Wherever you go, the image of this Higher Power is with you. Driving your car, God is sitting beside you on the front seat. Walking along the sidewalk, God is walking right next to you. Sitting at your desk, God is sitting on your lap. You take your idea or personification of God with you, everywhere you go. This method of prayer and meditation improves your conscious contact with God as you understand God and provides an objectified way of obtaining the knowledge of God's will for you and the power to carry that out.

I find when I take my Higher Power to work with me and keep God with me throughout the day, I gain the power not to work addictively, and this makes my time at work a blessing rather than a curse.

With my Higher Power by my side, my identity, validation, and escape from painful emotions no longer depend upon my occupational status or how hard and fast I work. My Higher Power gives me a healthy sense of identity and validation and a healthy way of coping with painful emotions that is exclusive of the kind of job I have or the amount of work I produce.

The rewards and freedom that result in being liberated

from the chains of addictive work are great. Seeing work as a pleasurable and productive activity, rather than a means to status, self-worth, and escape, makes one's life much more enjoyable. When work is placed in its proper perspective, as a means of earning the money we need to pay the bills and as a way to make a positive contribution to the society we live in, other areas of our lives like home, family, and play begin to obtain their rightful positions.

Even eating and sleeping, which normally take forty-five percent of our daily living time, become the blessings God intended them to be, when we keep work in its proper place.

Debtors Anonymous, Gamblers Anonymous, and The 12 Steps for Everybody are the three 12-Step programs that relate most closely to using the 12 Steps on the addiction to work. If there are no groups currently active in the area where you live, you can start a group of your own or you can simply proceed to work the 12 Steps on your workaholism on your own.

You can develop a 12-Step correspondence with others around the country who suffer from the addiction to work. There are all kinds of creative ways to work the 12 Steps on a particular addiction, and half the fun of recovery involves discovering and making use of these new and unique ways. One day at a time, we can let go of addictive work and live better lives for ourselves and those around us.

Chapter 18

PARANOIA

Like many of the previously discussed mental and emotional *intangible* addictions, paranoia has been with me as far back as I can recall. In the last chapter I defined paranoia as delusions of grandeur or persecution.

It's strange that this pathological condition should operate with such distinctly opposable lapses in reality: grandeur and persecution. The notion that we could mistakenly think either we're great personages or we're being wrongfully attacked by others seems like such a contradiction in logic and terms, but it is certainly consistent with the two-sided coin phenomenon of many addictions.

We addicts tend to be habituated to extremes. Either we work all the time or not at all. Either we gorge ourselves or starve ourselves. Either we love too much or not enough. We either/or ourselves to death.

A great figure in the field of psychology once called the alcoholic "His Majesty the Baby," and a great book on alcoholism describes alcoholics as overly sensitive, immature, and grandiose. So by the observation of other types of addictive behavior, it is not hard to accept that if we're suffering from paranoia, we either think we're Napoleon or we're being mistreated by the cleaning lady. Or, both.

From my perspective there are two kinds of paranoia, one generated by schizophrenia and the other by the borderline personality. Schizophrenic paranoia and borderline paranoia both germinate in a special combination of genetic, glandular, biochemical, and environmental origins, dependent upon each individual; however, there is a marked difference in the quality and duration of the psychotic episodes which result.

The schizophrenic paranoid loses touch with reality completely and for long periods of time (days, weeks, or months), while the borderline paranoid loses touch with reality only partially and for shorter periods of time (usually no longer than a few hours).

I don't know if schizophrenic paranoia can be treated with the 12 Steps or not. Most of the schizophrenic paranoids I've known have needed some form of medication to manage their disease. However, I do know that borderline paranoia is an addiction, which can be treated with the 12 Steps because this is my own personal experience.

I've lived with paranoia all my life to the extent that whenever I'm around other people, I basically feel that they don't like me, think I'm a jerk, don't want to be around me, and are probably planning to do me some kind of harm.

When I walk out onto the street or into a room, these are the thoughts and feelings, which naturally flood into my mind and body. I believe this paranoid condition comes from the terrible childhood relationship I had with my mother, another narcissistic, borderline individual, who often actually *was* out to get me.

Consequently, whenever I find myself in times of stress today as an adult (hunger, anger, loneliness, or fatigue) I transfer my childhood paranoid reactions onto the people and situations around me. My natural (or unnatural in this case) response when my defenses are down is to think that the people around me are thinking bad thoughts about me. I usually feel this way quite strongly with loved ones like my spouse and my children.

Once the neurological responses become set, the habit becomes fixed, and the addiction is in operation. When you react over and over again to stress by becoming suspicious that the people around you are persecuting you in some way, this behavior pattern becomes an addiction that you cannot stop, even if you want to.

Even though you know where it comes from, even though you know it's illogical and it's destroying your life and your relationships, you can't break the habit. One part of your brain tells you there's absolutely no reason at all to be paranoid, while the other part of your brain twists reality to make it look like you have every reason in the world to suspect and fear attack from those around you.

To vacillate back and forth between paranoia and reality, in and out of delusion, is a state comparable to the alcoholic who vacillates back and forth between drunkenness and sobriety.

Sometimes addictive paranoia manifests itself as an ongoing state of being mildly paranoid. This is the usual case for me when I enter a restaurant alone.

As I sit at the table, waiting for the waitress to take my order, I become apprehensive and impatient. I'm fearful she won't come soon so that I can eat. Or perhaps that she won't come at all. My anxiety, impatience, hunger, and loneliness immediately throw me into an incipient paranoid condition.

The normal person, sitting alone in a restaurant, feels lonely and perhaps isolated but ignores it. The paranoia junkie feels lonely, isolated, alienated, and persecuted.

Sitting there waiting for the waitress, I begin to feel that maybe she's not waiting on me because she doesn't like my looks. Maybe they (the management) want me to leave. They (the other customers) are all different from me. They're better dressed, they make more money, they're together, they're "real" people.

I'm just a phony. They can see right through me. They're probably talking about me and laughing at me right now out in the kitchen. I feel like getting up and leaving.

The rational part of my mind argues against this. Of course, the waitress doesn't dislike you! She's just busy. Everybody else is paying attention to themselves. Don't be so self-centered, relax! Look at your fingernails. You're all right.

Logic struggles to overcome the paranoia, but the addiction is too strong and the paranoia creeps back. The waitress comes and this time I'm sure she doesn't like me. She's not smiling. She wants me to leave. I give her my order anyway, and then when she leaves I start to use "judgmentalism" and criticism to defend against my paranoia.

She's nothing but a fat, dumpy broad. What am I worried about? This whole place is a flytrap. Look at the customers! They look like refugees from a nursing home. I'm all right. I'm the best thing they've got in this place.

But, indulging in one addiction (judgmentalism) never alleviates another (paranoia) for very long, and soon I am right back in the bag again, thinking inferior thoughts about myself and suspecting that the others in the room are thinking critical and judgmental thoughts about me. When my addiction to paranoia kicks in, there's no way out but the 12 Steps.

In kindergarten I played alone at one end of the playground, so that I didn't have to face those painful feelings of inferiority and paranoia when I was with the other kids. In grade school and high school, I desperately sought the company of companions I felt superior to, so I didn't have to suffer the paranoia I felt around those I perceived as superior to me.

After drinking alcoholically as a teenager for two years, I developed a full-blown paranoid delusion that I was the human guinea pig in a secret psychological experiment. I was also convinced that my mother was trying to kill me and that I was dying of cancer of the mastoid bone.

In the Army, aside from my friends, I felt that everybody else thought I was a jerk and hated me. As a classroom teacher and later a businessman, I was under the delusion that my students and employees were laughing at me and wanted me to fail.

There was rarely any evidence to support my paranoia all those years. The facts usually substantiated the exact opposite, that I was respected and well-liked by almost everyone. But my paranoid mind saw otherwise.

Is it any wonder that when I got to my first 12-Step meeting at the age of forty-two and saw that 2nd Step: "Came to believe that a Power greater than ourselves could restore us to sanity," that I was overjoyed by the prospect of being finally relieved of my paranoia?

And, yet, it was five full years before I got around to working the 12 Steps on my paranoia! I guess somehow I just naturally thought it would take care of itself. What a rude awakening. I had to reach a bottom on my paranoia, just like I had to reach a bottom on every other addiction on the menu of my addictive personality.

Paranoia has many of the same *payoffs* as anger, anxiety, depression, negative thinking, envy, guilt, obsession, and work. Indulging in paranoia enables me to feel anger toward the imagined perpetrators of my persecution, and then I can enjoy planning retaliatory action against them.

Paranoia gives me the cheap thrill of anxiety and the adrenalin rush of excitement, providing an escape from boredom. As a mental escape, it gives me attention, power, and control over my environment, as I use my imagination to manipulate the people and circumstances around me.

Paranoia is a substitute for me for guilt, inferiority, and low self-worth, allowing me to assuage these self-punishing addictions by experiencing the delusion that others are out to get me, when actually it's me and my inability to cope with normal feelings that's out to get me.

Paranoia was modeled for me as a child by both my parents and almost all of my relatives, who were chronically distrustful of everyone around them, convinced somehow that the whole world was out to get them if they turned their backs and gave it half a chance.

And, finally, paranoia gives me the neurological fix my

axons and dendrites (nerve endings) so desperately need to validate their programming, having been set so many years ago by genes, hormones, and cerebral observation to perform over and over again in a consistently paranoid fashion.

The bottom that finally impelled me to work all 12 Steps on addictive paranoia on a daily basis occurred when I had five and a half years of sobriety. I started living with my present (third) wife, and for our whole first year together in the same house I experienced intense attacks of paranoia whenever she was away from home.

Codependence and jealousy were triggering it off. If she was fifteen minutes late, I was convinced she was with another man. When the question of an old boyfriend came up, I was certain she was still seeing him. One part of my mind knew this was ridiculous, but the other part was certain my suspicions were well-founded.

We had terrible arguments over my paranoid delusions, she embarrassed and hurt that I would think anything like that about her, and I outraged and confused with the uncertainty which always accompanies incidents of jealous paranoia.

Borderline paranoia is always a no-win situation. If you're right and you are being persecuted, your life is a shambles. If you're wrong and you're not, your life is still a shambles anyway, because you're nuts.

During these excruciatingly painful fights with my wife, I became completely and totally demoralized by my paranoia. I became so sick and tired of being sick and tired of my paranoia I wanted to smash a hole in my skull with a hammer and rip out my brains with my own bare hands. It was a true bottom to indulging addictively in paranoia.

During many of these paranoid bouts I became so furious and distraught I threatened to move out, to call it quits. She'd go into the bedroom crying and close the door, and I'd lie out on the couch in a complete state of helpless agitation, trying to get to sleep.

But before I went to sleep I'd get down on my hands and knees and send up the following prayer: "Dear God, if you mean for this relationship to last you're going to have to intervene on our behalf, because I'm so sick and crazy with paranoia at this point that I'm not capable of doing anything other than destroying the marriage. If it is your will that this marriage survive, please help me."

With this action I was taking Steps 1, 2, 3, 6, 7, 10, and 11. I was admitting I was powerless over my paranoia and my life (marriage) had become unmanageable. I was coming to believe a Power greater than myself could restore me to sanity. I was turning my will and my life (marriage) over to the care of God as I understood God.

I was entirely ready to have God remove my paranoia. I was humbly asking God to remove my paranoia. I was continuing to admit that my paranoia was wrong. And I was seeking through prayer to improve my conscious contact with God, as I understood God, praying only for knowledge of God's will for my marriage and the power to carry that out.

After I said this little homemade prayer, I always felt better. I slept like a baby, somehow trusting in the 12 Steps and in the Higher Power to whom I was turning over my will, my life, and my marriage.

In the morning my paranoia was gone, and I was thinking rationally again. I apologized to my wife (Steps 8 and 9) and told her it was my addiction to paranoia, which had caused me to become abusive once more (Step 12). I assured her I was working the 12 Steps on my addiction to paranoia, and I thanked her for her understanding and patience. She too was working the 12 Steps on my paranoia and was able to detach with love from it and not take it so personally and seriously when I had a slip.

I wrote in my journal about my paranoia (Steps 4, 5, and

10), and I shared it with others at meetings and on the telephone (Step 12).

As time went by I stopped acting out on it. If my wife was fifteen minutes late and I chose to indulge in paranoia, I kept it to myself. I made a pact with myself: the only time I'll ever accuse my wife of sleeping with another man is if I catch her in the act. Otherwise, I'll keep my mouth shut and I'll work the 12 Steps on my paranoia.

And I'll "act as if." I'll act as if nothing is wrong, and I'm completely free of paranoia. Acting as if often creates the mental and emotional atmosphere to allow me to actualize what I really want. If I really want to be free of paranoia, and I act as if I am, I become so.

It's necessary for me to continue to work the 12 Steps on paranoia on a daily basis, otherwise the addiction returns. I'll be at work and boredom will set it off, and soon I'll be imagining my fellow employees really don't like me and are avoiding me.

I might get angry at something someone says or does, and then suspect that person is doing it on purpose to spite me or to hurt me. Feelings of inferiority and low self-worth often trigger off bouts of paranoia for me. Once I start to feel "less than," it's not long before I start to feel persecuted.

However, if I watch myself vigilantly with the 10th-Step Mind, inventorying my thoughts and feelings on an ongoing basis, I can usually catch myself before it goes too far. The other day was a good example.

During my morning meditation I began to develop a paranoid scenario in which I catch my wife sleeping with another man.

She tells me she was forced to do so. I tell her I'm leaving her and she puts up a fight, not wanting a divorce, and stabs me with a kitchen knife. Barely surviving, I live out the rest of my life as a bitter and lonely old bachelor, my one consolation being I'm finally free of all the backstabbing women in my life.

As you can see, there's a lot of room in this paranoid scenario for hurt pride, resentment, revenge, self-destruction, depression, and self-pity. The whole thing represents an addictive transference onto my wife of an unresolved childhood conflict with my mother, not that it makes much difference where it comes from since working the 12 Steps on it is the only method of recovery for a paranoia junkie like me.

My paranoid fantasy lasted about fifteen minutes before I was finally able to apply the 10th-Step Mind to it and to promptly admit I was wrong to continue to indulge in it any longer. It was the same as if I'd gone into a bar or donut shop and binged on alcohol or apple fritters for fifteen minutes, and then realizing what I'd done, I tried to get up and leave without drinking or eating any more.

But in this case, in order for me to get out of my binge of paranoia, I had to work the rest of the 12 Steps. I had to admit I was powerless over paranoia, that my life had become unmanageable, that there was a Power greater than myself who could restore me to sanity, and that I must turn my will, my life, and my paranoia over to that Power, which I call God.

In a very short period of time by working the 12 Steps on it, the paranoid scenario went away and I was able to take part in the rest of my day without suffering from paranoia.

The benefits of freedom from addictive paranoia are joy and happiness. It becomes possible to look upon family members, friends, and strangers as loved ones and companions, rather than as competitors and adversaries. Daily living becomes an enjoyable experience, instead of a mental and emotional battle.

The mind and the heart are able to perceive the surrounding environment as a friendly and open space, rather than a dangerous and hostile place. We begin to engage in the bright new world of the here-and-now, instead of wallowing helplessly and hopelessly in the dark bleak world of persecution and obsession.

Reality takes on a new meaning and a new truth for us, and we are able to laugh at the false substance of illusion and delusion. For those of us who've suffered from it for so many years, to shed the chains of addictive paranoia by working the 12 Steps is truly an amazing and wonderful experience.

Paranoia falls among those categories of intangible addictions, which are best confronted through working the 12 Steps in Emotions Anonymous, Emotional Health Anonymous, and The 12 Steps for Everybody. Attending the meetings of these 12-Step groups, we find the loving support and suggested direction that is so helpful to us in pursuing the path to personal freedom from paranoia.

Chapter 19

LOW SELF-ESTEEM & LOW SELF-WORTH

Who out there suffers from low self-esteem and low self-worth? If you've read this far in this book I should ask who among you does *not*, because if you've got the kind of addictive personality I've got, the chances are you're addicted to low self-esteem and low self-worth, too.

I believe these two addictions lie at the bottom of all the rest. Low self-esteem and low self-worth provide the breeding ground for all the other addictions. They are the "hole" we speak of when we talk about "fixing" or "filling" it; and we are addicted even to that hole.

I define self-esteem as the extent to which we respect ourselves and self-worth as the extent to which we value ourselves. The first is a measure of how we *treat* ourselves, and the second is a measure of how we *feel* about ourselves. Both are interdependent, and both are based critically upon what type of ego, or identity, we've formulated as children.

If we have a healthy ego (sense of self), then we have healthy self-esteem and healthy self-worth. If we have a damaged or fragmented ego, then we have unhealthy self-esteem and unhealthy self-worth.

Just like in the other two-sided coin addictions, the pathological or fragmented ego manifests itself in two or more extremes.

In the case of self-esteem, the damaged ego is at times hyper-inflated during periods of fantasy or achievement, resulting in feelings of grandiosity and superiority. At other times, such as periods of stress, failure, expectation, frustration, pain, or fear, the damaged ego is hyper-deflated or collapsed, resulting in feelings of helplessness and inadequacy. Some of us in 12-Step meetings describe ourselves as egomaniacs with inferiority complexes.

As for feelings of self-worth, when the damaged ego hyper-inflates we evaluate ourselves as "good." When the ego hyper-deflates or collapses, we evaluate ourselves as "bad."

Notice we don't relent from a continuous judgment of ourselves, and we don't integrate our evaluation. We are either good or bad; there is no in-between or moderation for those of us who suffer from addictive excesses. It's all either black or white.

Normal people growing up in functional households develop healthy egos and healthy identities. They like themselves and do not experience the extreme vacillation and ambivalence toward "self" that the dysfunctional household child experiences.

In the alcoholic codependent environment I grew up in, the ego and the identity lacked individuation and introjected the parents' low opinions of themselves and everyone around them. Anyone in my family with self-esteem, self-worth, or even self-confidence was vilified as being too big for his own britches or too smart for his own good.

Self-esteem was not rewarded. In fact, it was punished. You were insulted and abused if you acted like you felt good about yourself, and God forbid you should do anything to draw attention to yourself because the bigger you are, the harder you fall. I became habituated to low-self esteem and low self-worth by a familial system of rewards, punishments, and modeling.

When we are addicted to low self-esteem and low self-worth, we tend to be very self-destructive. Since we chronically consider ourselves as unworthy and bad people, we constantly feel as though we need to be punished.

Throughout the years I destroyed myself over and over again in all areas of my life, because I didn't respect myself or think I was worth anything. Whenever things were going well in my life, I booby-trapped them. I gave up, or squandered, marriages, families, houses, friends, careers, businesses, inheritances, and countless opportunities in all areas of my life.

As soon as it looked liked I was doing well, I'd pull the rug out from under myself and throw it all away. I just didn't feel worthy of anything good. I was *compelled* to destroy myself. The funny, or rather tragic, thing is I tended to romanticize the whole thing. I even wrote the following poem to my second ex-wife late one night in a drunken stupor toward the end of our marriage.

"The Reason"

There is a force inside of me
That makes me destroy myself
Over and over,
So I can rebuild myself
Over and over,
In new and better forms.
And the reason is you.

How I cried in my beer over that one! I pictured myself some sort of modern heroic phoenix, the mythical Egyptian bird that supposedly destroys itself in fire every five hundred years, only to rise from its own ashes renewed and strengthened.

The drama and self-pity I wrung from this notion was incredible. Little did I realize the actual "reason" for this bizarre self-destructive behavior was not my second ex-wife or my brave immortal spirit. The real reason was my addiction to low self-worth and the continuous pounding of self-destructive behavior with which I relentlessly punished myself.

For twenty-five years before I came to the 12-Step programs, I sought the reason for my low self-worth and self-destructive behavior in an exploration of my unconscious mind and the traumatic incidents in my early childhood, which I felt would somehow give me the answers I needed for relief, once rooted out.

I underwent psychotherapy, psychoanalysis, transactional analysis, Gestalt therapy, humanistic psychological strategies, primal therapy, EST, and transcendental meditation in an attempt to make the necessary breakthroughs, to unlock the secrets of the past which would enable me to become an integrated, healthy, and positively functioning human being.

During this time I learned about my unresolved conflicts with my mother and my resentful and envious competition with my father, but knowledge and insight alone were not sufficient to liberate me from my addiction to low self-esteem, low self-worth, and self-destructiveness. I found out what was wrong with me, but in order for me to change a much stronger force or power was necessary. I found that power finally in the 12 Steps of the 12-Step programs.

Before we look at how the 12 Steps work successfully on letting go of low self-esteem and low self-worth, let's examine the *payoffs* we get from indulging in these two extremely destructive addictions.

The addictive practice of low self-esteem and low self-worth triggers off anxiety, which in turn gives us an adrenalin rush and provides *excitement* in the form of fear in our lives. Low self-worth enhances the sense of drama in our lives. We become the unsung heroes, the underdogs, who we always identified with, the romantic figures who warrant pity and a kind of *perverse self-esteem.*

This provides us with a safe position to operate from, because it means we don't have to expect anything from ourselves but the worst. Since we're losers to begin with, nothing is really lost when we continue to fail. In fact, we have a license for failure. We can even feel "special" in our roles as unrespected and unworthy people. Thus, practicing low self-esteem and low self-worth gives us *attention*.

As long as we have low self-esteem and low self-worth, we feel we have the right to *envy and resent* those who've achieved something we haven't. I always saw myself as a righteous proletariat, a helpless member of the downtrodden working-class, struggling hopelessly against the vicious exploitation of the materialistic bourgeois landowners (even when *I* had a house with a swimming pool).

I was unaware that my political indignation was fueled primarily by low self-esteem and low self-worth, which made me feel that no one was really entitled to enjoy anything. My low self-worth actually gave me what I thought was a legitimate reason for *doing nothing*, a good portion of my life, but simply sitting around in an *agitated depression*, unable to move.

I'm certain that *paranoia* has been a major payoff for my long-standing addiction to low self-esteem and low self-worth. When my damaged ego indulged in the other side of the coin behavior and soared with a hyper-inflated idea of my own self-worth, pushing me to heights of *superiority*, I experienced those highs, those delusions of grandeur spoken of in the previous chapter on paranoia.

However, when the crash came and my damaged ego turned the coin over and slid me back into the hyper-deflated depths of low self-worth, I craved the feelings of *persecution* from others as a means of punishment and self-destruction. At those times the delusion that others were out to get me was based on my own desires to get myself, to destroy myself, because I felt I deserved it.

And, of course, the final payoff for any emotional excess, low self-esteem, low self-worth, or otherwise, is the *neurological fix* we get when our whole nervous system comes to experience that which we are so used to, that which we have been habituated to from an early age.

We only really feel comfortable, neurologically, when we

feel low self-worth. If we were to experience the feeling of healthy self-worth, our nervous systems wouldn't know how to react. It would make us feel uncomfortable.

And this is the insane paradox of the emotional addictions from which many of us suffer. That which makes normal people feel uncomfortable, makes us feel comfortable. And that which makes normal people feel comfortable makes us feel uncomfortable. We're wired in reverse! And often times we find that even though it seems entirely unbelievable, we actually crave pain rather than pleasure, because that is all we really know, that is all we're really used to.

Even after I reached the 12-Step programs and learned how to work the 12 Steps on other tangible and intangible addictions, I didn't reach a bottom on low self-esteem and low self-worth right away. In fact, low self-esteem and low self-worth seemed to be the last mental and emotional addictions I was ready to face.

There were many other defenses, or "cures," I had to try first before I was ready for the 12 Steps. First, I had to try to raise my self-esteem by getting my second ex-wife back. That didn't work. Then I had to try working in some prestigious jobs. That didn't work. Then I had to try becoming a rich and famous screenwriter. That didn't work. Then I had to try another marriage. That didn't work. Finally, when all else failed, I reached my bottom on low self-esteem and low self-worth, and it happened in a very simple and unimpressive way.

I was sitting in a 12-Step meeting one night with nine-and-a-half years of sobriety, and a woman who reminded me of my mother was talking about how there were some people in this world whom she simply did not like. She did not hate them. She did not resent them. She did not wish them ill. She simply did not *like* them.

Suddenly, I came to understand that this was the way my mother treated me. Whether or not she loved or hated me was of no consequence. She simply did not like me.

This realization lowered my physical resistance, and I came down with a horrible case of the flu. I was in bed for a whole week with nothing to do but to get in touch, in depth, with just how low my self-esteem and self-worth really were.

It filled me with awe. I couldn't see how I'd managed to avoid killing myself all these years with such low self-esteem and low self-worth. It was a sheer miracle that a person who devalued himself as much as I could have even made it to the age of fifty-two.

I got in touch with the great pain this low self-esteem and low self-worth had caused me all these years, and I began to develop some compassion, understanding, and acceptance of myself and who I am. I began to feel forgiveness, not only toward my mother, who really couldn't help how she felt about me, but also toward myself for being sick (codependent) enough to buy into her value system and to use it for my own all these years. I realized how much pain and suffering this had caused me, as well as others.

My denial system was broken, and I got in touch with how deeply I've been addicted to the low self-esteem and low self-worth that I was taught as a child. I became sick and tired of being sick and tired of it. Lying in that sick bed for a week, recovering from the flu, I finally got to the point where I'd had enough of low self-esteem and low self-worth.

And I don't believe I would have been ready to reach that point one day sooner than when it happened. I believe our Higher Powers give us what we get, only when we are really *entirely* ready to get it.

Of all the addictions I suffer from, I know of no other which is more in need of a Higher Power and the 12 Steps for recovery than low self-esteem and low self-worth. Self-esteem and self-worth are so closely connected with the ego, the identity, the "self" itself, that what we are up against is changing the *deepest* part of ourselves completely.

One well-known medical doctor expressed it as the need for a complete psychic change. In my experience, the only way to achieve such a dramatic personality change is to thoroughly practice the 12 Steps on a daily basis.

I must admit I'm powerless over my low self-esteem and low self-worth and my life has become unmanageable. I must come to believe a Power greater than myself can restore me to sanity and take away my low self-esteem and low self-worth, replacing them with a healthy self-esteem and a healthy self-worth. I must make a decision to turn my will, my life, and my low self-esteem and low self-worth over to the care of God as I understand God.

Working Step 4 and making a searching and fearless moral inventory of myself with respect to my low self-esteem and low self-worth is extremely important in the process of letting go of these two self-destructive addictions. I had to sit down and write extensively about my past life in terms of where, when, and how I had hurt myself and others with my low self-esteem and low self-worth.

It is not easy to bring up the wreckage of the past, but I've found from experience that if I don't, if I don't call up an accurate picture of the mental and emotional mistakes I've made, I am doomed to repeat them. Writing a Step 4 inventory helps me to realize that I'm really sick and tired of being sick and tired of low self-esteem and low self-worth. It helps me to become entirely ready (Step 6) to have God remove these two rapacious defects of character.

Avoiding the pain of a Step 4 inventory on my low self-esteem and low self-worth is merely allowing my toxic condition to slip back into a state of denial, from which I will find it easy once again to begin to indulge addictively in more low self-esteem and more low self-worth.

Admitting to God, to ourselves, and to another human

being the exact nature of our wrongs (Step 5) with respect to low self-esteem and low self-worth is also very important in getting ourselves into the *position* of letting go. We have to bring God or our idea of a Higher Power into this process in my estimation, or else the process simply won't work.

It doesn't matter what kind of concept of a Higher Power we want to entertain. It can be a traditional God, the 12-Step group we belong to, the Universe, or the County Sheriff's Department: anything we wish to concede is more powerful than we are.

We can be creative! This is our opportunity to create our *own* God, a God of *our* understanding. The reason it's important to have a Higher Power, any Higher Power we want, is that we need something to surrender to, to admit to, to turn our addiction(s) over to.

As long as we don't have any Power greater than ourselves, we continue to consider ourselves to be more powerful than anything else. And as long as we consider ourselves to be more powerful than anything else, we're doomed to continue making the same mistakes over and over again and being powerless to do anything about it.

Resentment, fear, and obstinacy are the three great stumbling blocks to choosing a Higher Power. Most of us carry a lifetime of resentment toward the word "God," and all that it stands for, because of our religious upbringing. We were mentally and emotionally abused by the God-concept of others, and thus we decided to throw out the concept of God for ourselves completely.

Many of us tried out a prayer once in a while, just to see if God really did exist, and when God didn't answer our prayers the way we wanted, we gained even deeper resentment and a more thorough resolve to banish God to the minds of those who were stupid enough to believe in It.

And as if resentment is not enough of a barrier for us to

place between ourselves and recovery, we allow a nagging fear of God to keep us from even considering the question of God with anything other than anger.

Anger toward God is our defense against that terrible fear, that self-centered fear that we will not get what we want, or that we will lose what we already have. What we really believe is, any Creator who could be vindictive enough to make the kind of mess we call our universe today must be a pretty dangerous Being to believe in.

What we actually find (those of us who have the willingness to choose a Higher Power and to design God the way we want) is that it's not our Higher Power we need to fear, but we ourselves. *We* are the ones who have ruined our lives over and over again with every addiction possible. A Higher Power has been trying to help us all along. We just haven't given It a chance.

Of course when does an addict really give *anything* a chance other than his or her own addiction? Obstinacy, that quality of being stubborn to the point of death (our own and everyone else's) is a trait which we often wear as a badge of honor. We may have lost everything else, but by God we'll stand by our right to be obstinate with respect to a Higher Power to the very end!

We'd rather be dead than give the Higher Power concept a chance. At least, then we can say we did it *our* way. Yes, resentment, fear, and obstinacy have kept us in the dark for a very long time with respect to God, and sometimes it takes some of us *years* before we are willing to let ourselves come out into the light.

I suppose compassion is the best we can do for those of us who are still so resentful, fearful, and obstinate that we refuse to believe there is no Power greater than ourselves in this universe.

Low self-esteem and low self-worth are treated in two

ways. First, it's necessary to work all 12 Steps on them on a regular basis, so we can let go of our addiction to them. Second, by working the 12 Steps on them daily, low self-esteem and low self-worth began to be transformed into healthy self-esteem and healthy self-worth through *action*.

By practicing the principles of the 12 Steps in all of our affairs, a self-esteem and a self-worth which do not need to vacillate between grandiosity and inferiority begin to form. By good orderly direction (G.O.D.), by right action, and by right living, we are gradually able to let go of our addiction to low self-esteem and low self-worth.

Those 12-Step spiritual principles of self-discovery, self-disclosure, forgiveness, acceptance, amends, vigilance, prayer, meditation, and working with others, which we strive to follow in our daily lives, begin working on us medicinally, healing our damaged egos and taking away the addiction to low self-esteem and low self-worth.

Life without low self-esteem and low self-worth is a glorious experience, like nothing I've ever known before. I've finally been able to enjoy my daily experiences and to be happy, something I never expected I'd ever be able to say. With a healthy self-esteem and a healthy self-worth, I can live constructively, rather than destructively, free of guilt and free of the need to punish myself and those around me.

This is not the way it is all the time. I have many moments when I slip back into low self-esteem and low self-worth. But if I work Step 10 on a continuous basis, I am able to catch myself before I go too far, and then working the rest of the 12 Steps I can let go of these addictions once again and experience the serenity and joy of living without them.

Emotions Anonymous, Emotional Health Anonymous, and The 12 Steps for Everybody are the 12-Step programs which apply themselves most directly to working the 12 Steps on low self-esteem and low self-worth.

A good way to recover from these two mental and emotional addictions is to start a 12-Step group of your own, so you can carry the message of the 12 Steps to those who still suffer from these addictions in your own home town.

We know of no other method, which will so thoroughly insure liberation from the chains of an addiction than that of working with those who still suffer from our own or other addiction(s). Let the joy of working Step 12 be yours today.

Chapter 20

EVERYTHING

Thus far we have discussed over twenty-five separate addictive behaviors – what they were like for me, what happened, and what they are like now that I work the 12 Steps on them. While writing this book I became amazed at just how many behaviors, thoughts, feelings, and activities have the capacity of becoming addictive. Before I discuss some more of them I would like to repeat what I mentioned earlier in the "Introduction" regarding my definition of addiction.

There are as many different ways to define addiction as there are people to do it. Physicians, attorneys, and even addicts themselves will come up with all kinds of definitions. None of them really mean much unless the addict *himself* believes he or she fits the definition and wants to do something about it. Everybody else in the world can insist that the addict's behavior is addictive, but if the addict himself doesn't agree and doesn't want to change, it simply doesn't matter.

Let's say, for example, that every evening for the past twenty years you've come home from work, slammed the screen door, kicked the dog, and punched the wall. People have tried to get you to stop this behavior for years, but you don't want to. It might bother your neighbors, the dog, and the other family members, but it doesn't bother you. They might say you're addicted to it, but *you* don't think so.

Even if you thought so, if you didn't want to change it wouldn't make any difference. And so the first ingredient to my definition of addiction is that the addict *admits* he is addicted and *wants* to change.

The second ingredient is just as critical. To return to the example above, let's say that because of your door-slamming, dog-kicking, wall-punching behavior, your neighbors start legal action against you, the dog runs away from home, your doctor tells you you're going to lose your hand, and your wife and children threaten to leave, if you don't stop.

So you try real hard and you stop. Then, by my definition you're not addicted. If you can refrain from a destructive behavior through your own will power alone, then you're not an addict. The second ingredient to my definition of addiction is that the addict *fails with every attempt of self-will* to give up his or her addiction.

What I'm saying, in effect, is that any definition of addiction which does not include the addict's *admission* of his addiction, his *willingness* to change, and his admission of his *powerlessness* is totally useless.

My definition of addiction demands that the basic elements of recovery (admission, willingness, and powerlessness) be present in the addict's thinking, or else the definition is only an academic speculation. Which brings us to the question of "good" addictions, as opposed to "bad" addictions.

Earlier in the book I stated that any behavior, thought, feeling, or activity that was destructive to oneself or others was excessive and, therefore, addictive behavior. It doesn't really matter if I apply this definition to the person who slams the screen door, kicks the dog, and punches the wall, because if he or she doesn't think it's destructive or excessive behavior, he or she isn't going to do anything about it.

In the same light, when someone accuses me of being addicted to the 12 Steps and the 12-Step meetings, I have to agree on one hand. On one hand, I'm hooked on the 12 Steps and the 12-Step meetings, because without them I'm unable to survive and would quite readily end up in the grave or in jail, I'm sure. I am addicted, or habituated, to the 12 Steps and the 12-Step meetings the same way I'm addicted to breathing, eating, and sleeping. I need them on a regular basis or I will die. These I would consider "good" addictions. They are *con-*

structive rather than *destructive*.

However, whether or not your addiction exists, whether or not you consider it good or bad, even whether or not you admit you're addicted and powerless, it all boils down to *whether or not you are willing to change*. If you are willing to change, and you have failed at *every other* attempt to change, then it is my belief and experience that the 12 Steps will work for you, if you *work* them. You might be able to identify with some of the possible addictions discussed below.

One of the most serious addictions in our society today is the addiction to abusing and being abused. There is, in fact, a 12-Step program which deals with a segment of this addiction called Parents Anonymous, for parents who are addicted to abusing their children. It's been shown that the 12 Steps are successful in helping the child-abusing parent to let go of this deadly addiction, once day at a time.

The media today are filled with news stories, documentaries, and dramatic presentations portraying the battering syndrome in terms of wife and child abuse and molestation. However, the fact is that this addiction to abusing and being abused exists in milder and much broader forms in all walks of our society.

Some people are addicted to insulting others and satisfy their craving for abusing by disguising their insults with humor, insisting they're only "kidding." Just as the alcoholic tries to disguise his addiction to alcohol by calling it a toast, a pick-me-up, an eye-opener, a before-dinner drink, or an after-dinner drink, the person addicted to abusing others calls it a joke, a suggestion, a reprimand, or even insists that the recipient deserves the abuse. This is the way the abuse-addict rationalizes his or her addictive behavior.

Usually people who are addicted to abusing or being abused grew up in abusive households. The abusive childhood environment is where the addiction began. As time goes by, the abuse-addict seeks out others who will take part in abusing and being abused. The addictive abuse can take the form of kidding, insulting, shouting, or actual physical hurting.

Some abuse-addicts are also addicted to sadism and get pleasure out of abusing others. Some abuse-addicts are addicted to violence and get their addictive *payoff* from violent behavior. This sometimes leads to an addiction to murder, which I will discuss in a subsequent paragraph.

It seems strange to think that some people can become addicted to being abused, but I would say that almost everyone who grew up in an alcoholic or otherwise dysfunctional household is addicted to being abused to some degree or another. As children we were abused on a regular basis. In some cases it was the only parental or fraternal treatment we knew. Often it was confused with love, because they told us: "I wouldn't do this to you if I didn't love you."

Consequently, we became habituated to abuse and found ourselves in our adult lives getting abused over and over again by our friends, loved ones, fellow employees, complete strangers, and even ourselves. Why did we remain in so many of these abusive situations if we were not addicted to it?

We always came up with some rationalization, some excuse for why we *had* to stay, but the truth is, we were addicted to it. In my case I was only able to escape this terrible addiction to being abused by working the 12 Steps on it. And even then I had to address the fact that I was addicted to self-abuse, too, in the form of being chronically accident prone, habitually self-sacrificing, and habitually placing myself in humiliating situations on a regular basis. Fortunately, the 12 Steps has worked on this, too.

Only *you* can decide if you are addicted to a particular behavior or not. And whether or not you decide one way or the other, it won't matter if you are not ready to *do* something about it. You might have tried cutting back or controlling what you think is a behavioral problem that's been getting you into trouble, but if you are a *true* addict in any area of your life, you will not be able to stop on your own. You'll find, as I did, that you need the help of the 12 Steps to do it.

All of us know at least one person (other than ourselves) who is compulsively obsessed over some behavior which seems quite harmless on the surface. Many of these obsessive people are addicted to reading, card games, competition, entertainment, excitement, or sports.

There are bookworms, pinochle fanatics, movie buffs, video game freaks, golfing enthusiasts, and football junkies. Some are addicted to playing; others are addicted to watching. I know someone who claims he watched a certain movie 487 times. He just couldn't get enough of it.

I know others whose spouses have threatened to divorce them if the zealot did not give up his stamp collection or her mahjongg club. Is there a child alive in America today who has not passed through an addiction to *television*?

Some of us have even stretched our own finances to the breaking point on some obsessive-compulsive hobby, endeavor, or pastime. Are these addictions? The answer is Yes. Do we want to give them up? The answer is usually No. However, if *your* answer is Yes to some addictive, obsessive-compulsive, or habitual problem in your life, it has been my experience that the 12 Steps will work on it.

Some people are addicted to *intellectual pursuits*. I know one woman who is addicted to going to college. She keeps getting degree after degree. Is this really an addiction? And, if so, is it a good one or a bad one? Only the woman can tell. But if she ever finds herself powerless over going to college and admits her life has become unmanageable (reaching a destructive bottom), then she'll find it is possible to obtain relief from her addiction to college by working the 12 Steps and going to 12-Step meetings.

For others it might be something as mundane as *sloppiness*. I know several people who have this addiction. Their room, or their whole house, looks like a tornado at a garage sale. If you point this out to them, they say, "What are you talking about?" Or else they get angry. Or else they say, "I know but I just can't seem to do anything about it."

They have all the reactions any self-respecting addict would have. However, it doesn't matter what anyone says to them or how hard we might try to change them. They will not be changed by others. And if they try to change themselves and are really true sloppiness-junkies, they won't make it. If this is their situation, the last resort is the 12 Steps.

I know people who are hooked on reminiscing about the *past*. All they do is think and talk about the past. They wallow in it. I happen to be one of them. If I'm not speculating about the future, I'm shuffling through the forest of the past, turning over rocks and old logs, seeing if I can find anything new to obsess over, or to add to an obsession I already have.

The past is a marvelous place to gain evidence for rationalizing present addictions. It's a wonderful place to escape to, to turn into a fantasyland that we think will fulfill all of the dreams and expectations that we don't see coming true in the reality of our lives today.

We can engage in this addiction to the past for as long as we want, but if the day ever comes when we are sick and tired of being sick and tired of digging up the past and we want to try living more in the present, the 12 Steps will alleviate this addiction. I know because I work the 12 Steps on my addiction to the past and they work.

There are some who are addicted to *perfectionism*. "If it's not worth doing right, it's not worth doing at all!" is the adage of the perfectionist. Others have an addiction to collecting *pets*. They walk with five dogs on a lease, or their whole house is overrun with cats. Still others go for *expensive things*: houses, cars, clothes, jewelry, and other toys.

I know many people who are habitual *savers*. They can't throw anything away. One man's basement is so packed with old bits of string and plastic containers he doesn't even have crawl space to get into it any longer. Are these addictions? Not if the person is not ready to change.

Pets and string might seem quite trivial compared to certain intangible addictions I've observed taking their toll on those who suffer from them. There's a whole package of addictions which I believe centers around *disorganization*.

Different people manifest this addiction in different ways. Some are habitually forgetful. Others are habitually confused. Some are chronically indecisive. Still others are always changing their minds. Some are hooked on irresponsibility or procrastination or uncertainty. Others just blame it on being scatterbrained.

But whatever you want to call it and whatever the results might be, I have found that these obsessive-compulsive behaviors fit the addictive model and, consequently, respond favorably to the 12 Steps and the 12-Step meetings.

Sleep is something I've seen people addicted to. I even experienced an addiction to sleep myself when I was in my 20's, sleeping from twelve to fifteen hours a day, despite my desire to wake up and get things done. It's probably connected to one form or another of depression.

I've observed people addicted to "geographics": changing jobs, relationships, apartments, and even cities on a regular basis. I'm also one of those. I pulled geographics addictively for the first forty-eight years of my life, including the first five years of my sobriety, driving back-and-forth across the country ten times.

One of the most insidious of my lifelong addictions has been to *speed*. I also call it "impatience." Impatience has shown itself in my behavior over the years in my addictions to amphetamines, speeding automobiles, eating fast, working in a frenzy, and playing golf too hurriedly.

I tend to hurry everything I do. I'm a "rushaholic." I can't stand to wait. Many times I have left a supermarket line or a doctor's waiting room because I couldn't cope with the frustration I experienced having to wait. My addiction to impatience has caused my life to become unmanageable in many ways.

I've messed up jobs by trying to do too many things at once. I've been a lousy lover because I had to hurry the act. I even had to quit writing screenplays because I couldn't stand the frustration of not being able to finish one in a week. Once I became aware of my addiction to impatience and my powerlessness over it, I was able to start working the 12 Steps on it and to experience some freedom from the bondage of this extremely destructive addiction.

Another killer addiction for me has been to *resentment*. Many pages in the literature of the book *Alcoholics Anonymous* are devoted to resentment. I have mentioned it in earlier chapters of this book. I bring it up again because it remains an ongoing addiction for me and one on which I need to work the 12 Steps diligently and continuously.

Resentment, when I indulge in it, gives me a sense of self-righteousness (perverse self-esteem), power, control (not letting others off the hook), hatred, revenge, superiority, and judgmentalism. I've held resentments for as long as nine years in the case of my second ex-wife and nineteen years in the case of my dead parents.

I will hold onto a resentment until my eyeballs bleed. I won't let go until I become so sick and tired of being sick and tired of the resentment that I fall on the floor kicking and screaming to become willing and able to work the 12 Steps on the resentment in question. Is this addiction to resentment? I think it fits my definition.

The area of our social behavior which I believe is most in need of the 12 Steps and the 12-Step meetings is criminal behavior. *Criminal behavior* consists of all forms of illegal activity, including murder, rape, robbery, burglary, assault, tax evasion, and even breaking the speed limit. If it's against the law, it's a crime, and I have seen overwhelming evidence that criminal behavior is an addiction.

On the night before Ted Bundy, the infamous serial murderer, was executed in Stark, Florida, he admitted he was addicted to pornography and murder and that his life had become unmanageable.

In my work in jails and prisons in the past, I have come into contact with many men who claimed that committing a crime, whatever it was, was the greatest high they'd ever experienced. The phrase "habitual offender" is the most accurate one to date in the criminal justice system. People who engage in criminal behavior on a regular basis are addicted to it. It's as simple as that.

The *payoffs* for criminal behavior include adrenalin rushes, power, control, anger, revenge, and the purgation of bad feelings like self-pity, fear, and low self-worth. More often than not, committing a crime is just another unsuccessful attempt at obtaining a fix, just another stab at trying to fill that hole in the gut that tells us we're not right, that something's wrong and we need something to fix it.

However, when the first crime wears off and we're not fixed, we're left with only one thing to do – commit another crime. And no matter how many times the crime is committed, it doesn't really achieve anything other than emphasizing the need to commit the crime, just one more time.

Given the knowledge that criminal behavior is addictive behavior, does this mean that we've solved the problem of crime in America today? Not any more than the knowledge that alcoholic behavior is addictive behavior is going to solve the problem of alcoholism in America today.

The only person who can stop criminal behavior is the criminal himself, and this will only be done when the criminal admits that he or she is powerless over his or her criminal behavior, that his life has become unmanageable, and that he is ready and willing to change. The 12 Steps are there for the criminals to use, if and when they are ready to work the 12 Steps on their addiction to crime.

Throughout this book and my examination of my own addictions, a common theme has appeared, and that common theme is the addiction to "self." The self, the ego, the identity, whatever we call it, is at the center of all of our addictions. That "hole" in the center of the self is what we are all trying to fill. Our character, our personality, our self is what we are made of, what dominates our behavior.

So many of us are addicted to selfishness, self-centeredness, self-consciousness, self-doubt, self-destruction, self-pity, and low self-esteem. We never seem to get enough of *self*. I believe the addiction to self is the master addiction, the addiction upon which all the others rest. As long as we remain all wrapped up in ourselves, we are chained inside a prison that keeps us from knowing anything at all about true happiness, serenity, or joy.

The way out of the addiction to self is through working the 12 Steps and going to 12-Step meetings. The spiritual principles of the 12 Steps are capable of breaking through the addiction to self.

Awareness, faith, surrender, self-discovery, self-disclosure, forgiveness, acceptance, amends, vigilance, prayer, meditation, and working with others – these are the tools we can use to let go of self and to live a life of joy and love. I believe that freedom from the addiction to self is the greatest happiness we can attain, and my own personal experience for short-lived moments bears this out.

That feeling of true love for God, ourselves, and other human beings comes when we step *outside* of self, and *unselfish* love is the only thing I've ever discovered that really fills that hole in my gut, the hole I've been trying to fix all these years with my addictions.

To paraphrase a few sayings from the 12-Step programs, this book is for those who want it, not those who need it. Take what you like and leave the rest. If you see how my experience can benefit you, make use of it.

If you have your own answers, that's all right, too. There are many paths to the top of the mountain. Whichever road you choose, good luck. You'll find *me* on the path of the 12 Steps and the 12-Step meetings and workshops. They work if we work them.

If you have any questions about working the 12 Steps or anything else in the above, write to: *The 12 Steps for Everybody, P.O. Box 444, Pacific Palisades, CA 90272; call 310-428-0904, e-mail info@12stepsforeverybody.org; or visit www.12stepsforeverybody.org.*

I

POSSIBLE ADDICTIVE BEHAVIORS

There may be some confusion as to what constitutes an "addiction." In the "Introduction," the statement is made: "...all irrational behaviors that are done repeatedly, over and over, can be called *addictions*." Of course, you have to ask yourself: Is the behavior, feeling, or action that I am habitually experiencing causing any negative consequences in my life? Take a look at the following list to see if you find anything there that is causing you enough problems in your life to warrant working the 12 Steps on it.

Abandonment
Abuse
Abusing
Accidents
Adversity
Advice
Aggression
Alcohol
Alienation
Ambivalence
Amusement
Anger
Anxiety
Apologizing
Approval
Arrogance
Astrology
Attack
Attention
Battering
Beliefs
Blaming
Books
Borrowing
Bullying
Busy Work
Card Games
Caretaking
Chronic Illness
Clutter
Codependence
College
Comparing
Competitiveness
Complaining
Compulsion
Control
Criminal Behavior
Criticism
Cynicism
Debt
Depression
Despair
Dishonesty
Disorganization
Distrust
Doormatism
Dreams
Drugs
Ego
Either/Or Thinking
Emotions
Entertainment
Envy
Erratic Mood Swings
Escape
Excitement
Expectations

Expensive Things
Explaining
Family Members
Fantasy
Fanaticism
Fear
Food
Forgetting
Frustration
Future-Tripping
Gambling
Games
Geographics
Giving
Gluttony
Gossip
Greed
Guilt
Hangovers
Hatred
Headaches
Health Foods
Helping
Helplessness
Homicidal Ideation
Honesty
Humiliation
Humor
Hypochondria
Immaturity
Impatience
Impotence
Impurity
Inadequacy
Indecisiveness
Inferiority
Ingratitude
Insecurity
Intolerance
Irresponsibility
Irritation
Isolation
Judging
Loneliness
Love
Low Self-Esteem
Low Self-Worth
Lust
Machismo
Malingering
Masochism
Money
Movies
Neatness
Negative Thinking
Neurotic Behaviors
Nicotine
Nudity
Numerology
Obsession
Obstinacy
Overacting
Overachievement
Overconfidence
Overdoing
Overdosing
Overdrawing
Overindulging
Overpowering
Overprotection
Overreaching
Oversensitivity
Pain
Paranoia
Past
People
People-Pleasing
Perfectionism
Persecution
Pessimism
Pets
Physical Exertion
Pleasure
Pornography
Possessiveness
Poverty
Prejudice
Pride
Problem-Solving
Procrastination
Prostitution
Radio
Reacting
Rebelliousness
Rejection
Relationships
Religion
Repression
Resentment
Revenge

Sacrifice
Sadism
Sadness
Sarcasm
Satisfaction
Saving Things
Security
Self
Self-Consciousness
Self-Doubt
Self-Esteem
Self-Destruction
Self-Pity
Self-Righteousness
Selfishness
Sex
Shame
Shyness
Significant Others
Sleep
Sloth
Speed
Spending
Spite
Sports
Stinginess
Stress
Stubbornness
Suicidal Ideation
Talking
Television
The Telephone
Therapy
Time
Transference
Unhappiness
Vicarious Thrills
Victimization
Violence
Weakness
Winning
Work

* * * * * * *

Perhaps one or more of these traits are repeatedly affecting your life in a negative way. Experience shows that working the 12 Steps will bring positive results and relief.

In "Appendix II," one method of working the 12 Steps on any addiction of habitual behavior is described.

In "Appendix IV," an additional method of working the 12 Steps on anything is described.

"Appendix III" describes how you can start your own 12-Step meeting.

"Appendix V" gives a list of some 49 12-Step and/or Anonymous programs that you can contact to help you work the 12 Steps.

If you have any questions about working the 12 Steps or anything else in the above, *call 310-428-0904, e-mail info@12steps-foreverybody.org; or visit www.12steps-foreverybody.org.*

II

HOW TO WORK THE 12 STEPS

The question often comes up, how do we work the 12 Steps? The answer is simple: *Read Them, Write Them, Think Them, and Recite Them.* Whenever you are troubled day or night with an addiction or habitual problem, you simply:

A. *Read silently to yourself through each of the 12 Steps, substituting your addiction or habitual problem where it applies.* For example, let's say you have the desire to smoke a cigarette. You take a sheet of paper with the 12 Steps on it and *read* through each Step, substituting the word "cigarettes" as your addiction.

1. I admit I am powerless over cigarettes and my life has become unmanageable. (Remember all of the ways you tried to quit cigarettes and failed. Remember all of the ways your life has become unmanageable due to cigarettes.)

2. I come to believe that a Power greater than myself can restore me to sanity and take away my desire to smoke cigarettes. (Think about the things that God has done for you during your lifetime.)

3. I make the decision to turn my will, my life, and my desire to smoke cigarettes over to the care of God as I understand God. (You get to define "God" in your own terms and with your own concept.)

4. I make a searching and fearless moral inventory of myself with respect to cigarette smoking. (Here you

would take a pencil and a piece of paper and write down all the times in your life when cigarette smoking has caused you and the people around you problems. Don't forget the smoky clothes, the cleaning bills, the holes in the sweaters, the bronchitis, the people you've offended, the times when you were too winded to play sports, the money you've spent on cigarettes. Get it all down in writing. Don't leave out anything.)

5. I admit to God, to myself, and to another human being the exact nature of my wrongs with respect to cigarette smoking. (Here you call or see somebody who has the time to listen, and you read to them the material you've written down for Step 4. They'll benefit immensely from hearing your 4th Step on cigarettes, because they can apply it to their *own* addiction or habitual problem.)

6. I am entirely ready to have God remove all my defects of character with respect to cigarette smoking.

7. I humbly ask God to remove my shortcomings with respect to cigarettes. (At this point get down on your knees and ask God to remove your obsession to smoke cigarettes, if it is God's will.)

8. I make a list of all persons I have harmed with my cigarette smoking and become willing to make amends to them all. (Here you would take a pencil and a piece of paper and write down all the people you've harmed. Don't forget the people you regularly exposed to exhaled and burning cigarette smoke,

thereby endangering them to bronchial problems, flu, and lung cancer. And how about the people you've accidentally burned with lighted cigarettes? Don't forget the cigarette smoke you leave in other people's clothes and automobiles because they have to pay to have that cleaned out, too.)

9. I make direct amends to such people I've harmed with my cigarette smoking wherever possible, except when to do so would injure them or others. (Start contacting those people and telling them you're sorry for the inconvenience, financial disbursement, and health endangerment your cigarette smoking has caused them in the past.)

10. I continue to take personal inventory with respect to my cigarette smoking and when I am wrong I will promptly admit it. (Make sure you do this. Promptly admit to yourself right now that you are wrong to desire a cigarette and that you would be insane to smoke one. Admit that you are offending yourself and everyone around you when you smoke cigarettes, not to say that you are endangering your own life as well as the lives of your loved ones.)

11. I seek through prayer and meditation to improve my conscious contact with God as *I understand God*, praying only for knowledge of God's will for me with respect to cigarette smoking and the power to carry that out. (Sit for a few moments and meditate, breathing in and out deeply and evenly. Do you think it is God's will for you to fill your lungs with putrid cigarette smoke? Do you think it is God's will that you endanger your own life and the lives of others?)

12. Having had a spiritual awakening as the result of these steps with respect to cigarette smoking, I will try to carry this message to others and to practice these principles in all my affairs. (Take this moment to telephone a fellow recovering smoker and to share with this person your experience, strength, and hope with respect to giving up cigarette smoking. You cannot free yourself from the obsession to smoke cigarettes if you do not work with others. You cannot keep recovery if you do not give it away.)

The chances are that if you have diligently followed the above instructions, reading silently through each of the 12 Steps with respect to your cigarette smoking, you will have lost the desire to smoke a cigarette at least momentarily. If you have not, then start from the beginning and work through the 12 Steps again, this time *writing* them *all* out on a piece of paper. Follow the example below regarding anger.

B. *Write down each of the 12 Steps, substituting your addiction or habitual problem where it applies.* If you are an anger junkie then take a sheet of paper and *write* down each Step, substituting the word "anger" as your addiction.

1. I admit I am powerless over my anger and my life has become unmanageable.

2. I come to believe that a Power greater than myself can restore me to sanity and take away my anger.

3. I make the decision to turn my will, my life, and my anger over to the care of God as I understand God.

Go through *all* 12 Steps, *writing* each down on a piece of paper with respect to your chronic anger, making sure to take the specific actions described above for Steps 4, 5, 7, 8, 9, 10, 11, & 12. *Action* is a key factor in working the 12 Steps, and you probably won't experience relief from your particular addiction or habitual problem until you take *action*. The more action you take, the more relief you will experience.

After *reading* each of the 12 Steps silently to yourself and *writing* each down on a piece of paper, if you are still suffering from your particular addiction or habitual problem, go through each of the 12 Steps again, this time *thinking* them to yourself. This time we'll use "depression" as an example.

C. *Think each of the 12 Steps to yourself, substituting your addiction or habitual problem where it applies*. If you are a chronic depressive, then substitute the word "depression" as your addiction.

   1. I admit I am powerless over my depression and my life has become unmanageable.
   2. I come to believe that a Power greater than myself can restore me to sanity and take away my depression.
   3. I make the decision to turn my will, my life, and my depression over to the care of God as I understand God.

Go through *all* 12 Steps, *thinking* each one silently to yourself with respect to your excessive depression, making sure to take the specific actions described above for Steps 4, 5, 7, 8, 9, 10, 11, & 12. After *reading* each of the 12 Steps silently to yourself, *writing* each one down on a piece of paper, and *thinking* each one silently to yourself, if you are still suffering from your particular addiction or habitual problem, go through each of the 12 Steps again, this time *reciting* them out loud. This time grief over the death of a loved one will be an example.

D. *Recite each of the 12 Steps out loud, substituting your addiction or habitual problem where it applies*. If you are grieving excessively (problematically) over the loss of someone you love, then substitute the word "grief" as your addiction.

1. I admit I am powerless over my grief and my life has become unmanageable.

2. I come to believe that a Power greater than myself can restore me to sanity and take away my grief.

3. I make the decision to turn my will, my life, and my grief over to the care of God as I understand God.

Go through *all* 12 Steps, *reciting* each one out loud with respect to your grief, making sure to take the specific actions described above for Steps 4, 5, 7, 8, 9, 10, 11, & 12. By now you must realize that *repetition* is very important in successfully working the 12 Steps on your addiction or habitual problem. The answer is simple: *Read Them, Write Them, Think Them, and Recite Them*, whenever you are troubled day or night with an addiction or habitual problem.

Sometimes it is necessary to work the 12 Steps over and over again throughout the day and night in order to experience just a modicum of relief from the pain of the addiction or habitual problem to which we are attached. These habitual attachments take years to form, and sometimes they take years to release. Pray "ceaselessly," as one spiritual leader once put it.

We have found that if you persist over the days, months, and years in a consistent practice of working the 12 Steps, you will find great joy and piece of mind. You will gain the power of choice, the power to choose *not* to smoke that first cigarette, *not* to take that first drink of excessive anger, *not* to wallow in that first wave of depression, or *not* to obsess over that first feeling of grief.

You will learn to say "no" to any addiction or habitual problem you have really had enough of, when you have *truly* had your fill of it, and you consistently *persist* in working the 12 Steps on it. Every time to choose *not* to indulge in an addictive thought, feeling, or act, you will get a spiritual lift. Your mind will gain peace and contentment. Your body will relax and become comfortable.

You will be able to look around and see the trees, the colors, the unique movements of the children and the animals in your world. You will take a new interest in things you did not notice before. The universe will amuse and delight you. A great clarity will emerge. You will receive insights of all kinds about all kinds of things. A sense of purpose and direction will overtake you.

You will know that you are all right just the way you are and that all is right with the world. The more you work the 12 Steps and the more addictions and habitual problems you give up, the more spiritual rewards you will receive. This is not a duty, an obligation, or a responsibility. It is merely a fact.

If you have any questions about working the 12 Steps or anything else in the above, write to: *The 12 Steps for Everybody, P.O. Box 444, Pacific Palisades, CA 90272; call 310-428-0904, e-mail info@12stepsforeverybody.org; or visit www.12stepsforeverybody.org.*

III

HOW TO START A 12-STEP MEETING

If you have identified with any of the materials in this book and would like to start working the 12 Steps on your own addictions, look in your local telephone directory for the 12-Step programs you are interested in. You can also consult the Internet and/or the list of some 49 12-Step and Anonymous programs in "Appendix V."

After seeking an established 12-Step organization or self-help support group, if you cannot find one you like, you are free to start your own. The best place for a meeting is a church, school, hospital, treatment center, community center, bank community room, civic organization, restaurant, or private home. Pick some place that will let you meet rent free, until your basket donations are large enough to pay rent.

Distribute fliers about your meeting to churches, schools, hospitals, libraries, community centers, Laundromats, and supermarket bulletin boards. Write press and calendar releases about your meeting and circulate them to the community events section of your local newspapers and shoppers. Post your meeting free-of-charge on craigslist.com, the Internet website.

You might want to start a 12 Steps for Everybody (TSE) discussion meeting or 12-Step writing workshop. The 12 Steps for Everybody is a 12-Step program for all those who wish to work the 12 Steps on anything and everything. The only requirement for membership is a desire to work the 12 Steps, or to help someone else to work the 12 Steps, on anything. Everyone is welcome, including members of all other 12-Step programs, Anonymous programs, and self-help support groups.

Below is the format for a TSE 12-Step writing meeting, the

Serenity Prayer, the 12 Steps, and the 12 Traditions.

T.S.E. FORMAT:

At 7:00 p.m. (or whatever time), Leader reads: "Welcome to the regular (day of week) meeting of 'The 12 Steps for Everybody.' My name is __________, and I am powerless over whatever."

Leader reads aloud: "The 12 Steps for Everybody is a fellowship of men and women who share their experience, strength, and hope that they may solve their individual problems and help others to work the 12 Steps on anything. The only requirement for membership is a desire to work the 12 Steps, or to help someone else to work the 12 Steps, on anything. There are no dues or fees for T.S.E. membership; we are self-supporting through our own contributions. T.S.E. is not allied with any sect, denomination, politics, organization, or institution; does not wish to engage in any controversy, neither endorses nor opposes any causes. Our primary purpose is to work the 12 Steps on anything."

Leader reads aloud: "The format of this meeting is that we go around the room, starting on my left, each sharing for 2 - 3 minutes on a particular problem on which he or she would like to work one or more of the 12 Steps today or tonight. We will then each write on one or more of the 12-Step Questions or Worksheets for approximately 20 minutes, after which we will each read aloud what we wrote. In the time remaining, we will open it up for sharing and discussion."

Leader indicates person on left to share the individual problem(s) he or she is going to write about today or tonight. After everyone has shared what they are going to write about,

Leader reads aloud: "We will now write for 20 minutes."

After 20 minutes of writing, Leader reads aloud: "Starting on my left each person will now read aloud what he or she has written."

After each person reads their writing, Leader reads aloud: "That's all the time we have for writing this evening. The meeting is now open for individual sharing. We ask that there be no cross talk or commenting on another person's writing or sharing."

At 7:55 p.m. (or 55 mins. after start) Leader reads aloud: "That's all the time we have for sharing today or tonight. Let's give each other a hand." (*Applause.*) "We have no dues or fees, but we do have rent." (*Pass the basket.*) "Are there any Secretary's announcements?"

Secretary reads aloud: "You are welcome to write on any of the 12-Step Questions or Worksheets during the week and to bring them to read aloud at the next meeting, if time permits. Let's give our leader a hand." (*Applause.*) "And now back to our leader."

Leader reads aloud: "To close the meeting, I would like to ask __________ to lead us in the Serenity Prayer."

THE SERENITY PRAYER: "God, grant me the serenity to accept the things I cannot change, the courage to change the things I can, and the wisdom to know the difference."

(If you so desire, you can read aloud either or both "The 12 Steps" and/or "The 12 Traditions" as printed below at any time during the meeting format.)

THE 12 STEPS:

1. We admitted we were powerless over *whatever* – that our lives had become unmanageable.
2. Came to believe that a Power greater than ourselves could restore us to sanity.
3. Made a decision to turn our will and our lives over to the care of God, as we understood God.
4. Made a searching and fearless moral inventory of ourselves.
5. Admitted to God, to ourselves, and to another human being the exact nature of our wrongs.
6. Were entirely ready to have God remove all these defects of character.
7. Humbly asked God to remove our shortcomings.
8. Made a list of all persons we had harmed, and became willing to make amends to them all.
9. Made direct amends to such people wherever possible, except when to do so would injure them or others.
10. Continued to take personal inventory and when we were wrong promptly admitted it.
11. Sought through prayer and meditation to improve our conscious contact with God as we understood God, praying only for knowledge of God's will for us and the power to carry that out.
12. Having had a spiritual awakening as the result of these steps, we tried to carry this message to others, and to practice these principles in all our affairs.

THE 12 TRADITIONS:

1. Our common welfare should come first; personal recovery depends upon T.S.E. unity.
2. For our group purpose there is but one ultimate authority – a loving God as God is expressed in our group conscience. Our leaders are but trusted servants; they do not govern.
3. The only requirement for T.S.E. membership is a desire to work the 12 Steps, or to help someone else to work the 12 Steps, on anything.
4. Each group should be autonomous except in matters affecting other groups or T.S.E. as a whole.
5. Each group has but one primary purpose – to carry its message to anyone who wishes to work the 12 Steps on anything.
6. A T.S.E. group ought never endorse, finance, or lend the T.S.E. name to any related facility or outside enterprise, lest problems of money, property, and prestige divert us from our primary purpose.
7. Every T.S.E. group ought to be fully self-supporting, declining outside contributions.
8. The 12 Steps for Everybody should remain forever non-professional, but our service centers may employ special workers.
9. T.S.E., as such, ought never be organized; but we may create service boards or committees directly responsible to those they serve.
10. The 12 Steps for Everybody has no opinion on outside issues; hence the T.S.E. name ought never be drawn into public controversy.
11. Our public relations policy is based on attraction rather than promotion; we need always maintain personal anonymity at the level of press, radio, TV, and films.

12. Anonymity is the spiritual foundation of all our traditions, ever reminding us to place principles before personalities.

(The 12 Traditions are adapted and reprinted with permission of Alcoholics Anonymous World Services, Inc.)

If you have any questions about finding or starting your own 12-Step meeting or workshop or anything else in the above, write to: *The 12 Steps for Everybody, P.O. Box 444, Pacific Palisades, CA 90272; call 310-428-0904, e-mail info@12stepsforeverybody.org; or visit www.12stepsforeverybody.org.*

IV

T.S.E. 12-STEP WRITING WORKSHOP QUESTIONS

Write on any one or more of the following 12-Step questions for 20 minutes or more and then read aloud what you have written to the group or to another individual. Blank = any thing, person, place, habit, addiction, illness, thought, emotion, or defect of character in your life that is causing you problems. For more information, call 310-428-0904, contact info@12stepsforeverybody.org, or visit www.12stepsforeverybody.org.

(The Twelve Steps are adapted and reprinted with permission of Alcoholics Anonymous World Services, Inc. The questions are reprinted with permission of The 12 Steps for Everybody, Inc.)

Step 1: *We admitted we were powerless over whatever – that our lives had become unmanageable.*

Do you realize that you are powerless over *blank* and that your life has become unmanageable?

a) List all of the ways that you have attempted, and failed, to control *blank*.

b) List all of the ways in which your life has become unmanageable due to *blank*.

c) Describe how your life would be, if you did not have *blank*.

Step 2: *Came to believe that a Power greater than ourselves could restore us to sanity.*

Have you come to believe that a Power greater than yourself can restore you to sanity and take away your *blank*?

a) Discuss what makes you believe that your Higher Power can restore you to sanity and take away *blank*.

b) Discuss any reservations that you have, regarding your Higher Power's ability to restore you to sanity and take away *blank*.

c) Discuss the attributes and characteristics of your Higher Power.

Step 3: *Made a decision to turn our will and our lives over to the care of God, as we understood God.*

Have you made the decision, on a daily basis, to turn your will, your life, and *blank* over to the care of God, as you understand God?

a) Discuss what you do on a daily basis to turn your will, your life, and *blank* over to the care of God, as you understand God.

b) Discuss what you do *not* do, but *should* be doing, on a daily basis to turn your will, your life, and *blank* over to the care of God.

c) Discuss examples of incidents in which you have turned your will, your life, and/or *blank* over to the care of God, and it has benefited you.

Step 4: *Made a searching and fearless moral inventory of our-*

selves.

Have you made a searching and fearless moral inventory of yourself regarding <u>*blank*</u>?

a) List your resentments, including who or what you resent, why you resent them or it, how it affects you and your life, your prayer that God gives you patience, tolerance, and compassion toward the person or thing, your prayer that God removes your anger toward the person or thing, and your part, or mistake, regarding your resentment toward the person or thing.

b) List all of your fears, including who or what you fear, why you have the particular fear, how it affects you and your life, and your prayer that God removes your fear and directs you as to what God would have you be.

c) List any selfish or hurtful sexual behavior you have done in the past, including how it has affected you and others, and your prayer that God removes your harmful sexual behavior in the future and directs you as to what God would have you be regarding your sexual behavior.

<u>**Step 5**</u>: *Admitted to God, to ourselves, and to another human being the exact nature of our wrongs.*

Have you admitted to God, to yourself, and to another human being the exact nature of your wrongs (defects of character, shortcomings)?

a) Make a list of the exact nature of your wrongs (defects of character, shortcomings).

b) List what actions you plan to take regarding these wrongs (defects of character, shortcomings).

c) List how you would like to behave in the future regarding your wrongs (defects of character, shortcomings).

Step 6: *Were entirely ready to have God remove all these defects of character.*

Are you entirely ready to have God remove all of your defects of character?

a) Make a list of all your defects of character that you are *entirely* ready to have removed.

b) Make a list of all your defects of character that you are **not** *entirely* ready to have removed.

c) Describe the reasons why you want to hold onto the defects of character in column 6b.

Step 7: *Humbly asked God to remove our shortcomings.*

Have you humbly asked God to remove your shortcomings?

a) Write out a prayer for each shortcoming that you are *entirely* ready to have removed, humbly asking God to remove it.

b) Write you a prayer for each shortcoming that you are **not** *entirely* ready to have removed, humbly asking God to make you *ready* to have it removed.

c) Describe how you would be *without* the shortcomings that you have prayed to have removed.

Step 8: *Made a list of all persons we had harmed, and became willing to make amends to them all.*

Have you made a list of all persons you have harmed and become willing to make amends to them all?

a) Make a list of all persons you have harmed and to whom you are *now* willing to make amends.

b) Make a list of all persons you have harmed and to whom you are *not yet* willing to make amends.

c) Discuss why you are not yet ready to make amends to those persons you listed in Column 8b.

Step 9: *Made direct amends to such people wherever possible, except when to do so would injure them or others.*

Have you made direct amends to such people wherever possible, except when to do so would injure them or others?

a) Using old records, telephone books, people you know how to contact, and the Internet, tell how you plan to seek out the persons listed in *Step 8a* above and make direct amends to them wherever possible, except when to do so would injure them or others.

b) Write out and recite a prayer to God to make you willing to make direct amends to each person listed in *Step 8b* above, except when to do so would injure them or others.

c) Describe how it makes you feel to be unwilling to make

amends to the persons listed in *Step 8b* above.

Step 10: *Continued to take personal inventory and when we were wrong promptly admitted it.*

Have you continued to take personal inventory regarding the practice of your defects of character, and when you are wrong promptly admitted it?

a) Discuss all of the incidents and situations during the past week, when you have practiced your defect(s) of character.

b) Discuss all of the incidents and situations during the past week, when you have promptly admitted you were wrong when you practiced your defect(s) of character.

c) Discuss how you would *like* to act and behave in future incidents and situations without practicing those defects of character.

Step 11: *Sought through prayer and meditation to improve our conscious contact with God as we understood God, praying only for knowledge of God's will for us and the power to carry that out.*

Have you sought through prayer and meditation to improve your conscious contact with God, as you understand God, praying only for knowledge of God's will for you and the power to carry that out?

a) List all of the incidents and situations during the past week, when you have sought (or *should have* sought) through prayer and meditation to improve your conscious contact with God, praying only for knowledge of God's will for you and the power to carry that out.

b) Describe the various forms of prayer and meditation you have used in certain incidents and situations during the past week.

c) Describe any positive results you have had through prayer and meditation during the past week.

Step 12: *Having had a spiritual awakening as the result of these steps, we tried to carry this message to others, and to practice these principles in all our affairs.*

Have you had a spiritual awakening as the result of these steps, and are you trying to carry this message to all those who wish to work the 12 Steps on *anything*, and to practice these principles in all your affairs?

a) Describe any thoughts or feelings you have had regarding a spiritual awakening you have experienced, as the result of these steps.

b) Describe the ways in which you have tried to carry this message to all those who wish to work the 12 Steps on *anything*.

c) Discuss what these "spiritual principles" are and how you practice them in all your affairs.

V

OTHER 12-STEP PROGRAMS

It is estimated there are over 500 12-Step, anonymous, and self-help programs and support groups throughout the world today. We have listed 49 below.

ADD Anonymous – If you have a problem with ADD.
http://members.aol.com/addanon/

Adult Children of Alcoholics – If you are the adult child of an alcoholic or a dysfunctional family.
P.O. Box 3216
Torrance, CA 90510
310-534-1815; info@adultchildren.org

Al-Anon – If you have a family member or friend who has a problem with alcohol.
1600 Corporate Landing Parkway
Virginia Beach, VA 23454-5617
888-425-2666
Al-Anon Family Groups of Southern California
4936 Lankershim Blvd.
North Hollywood, CA 91601
818-760-7122; centraloffice@alanonla.org

Alcoholics Anonymous – If you have a problem with alcohol.
A.A. General Service Office
Box 459, Grand Central Station
New York, NY 10163
212-870-3400
Los Angeles Central Office of A.A.
4311 Wilshire Blvd., #104
Los Angeles, CA 90010
800-923-8722; lacoaa@aol.com

All Addictions Anonymous – If you have a problem with all addictions.
416-468-8603; info@alladdictionsanonymous.com;
www.alladdictionsanonymous.com

Chemically Dependent Anonymous – If you have a problem with chemical dependency.
P.O. Box 423
Severna Park, MD 21146
888-232-4673

Clutterers Anonymous – If you have a problem with clutter or hoarding.
www.cluttersanonymous.net

Co-Anon Family Groups – If you have a family member or friend who has a problem with cocaine.
P.O. Box 12722
Tucson, AZ 85732-2722
520-513-5028 or 800-898-9985; info@co-anon.org

Cocaine Anonymous – If you have a problem with cocaine.
3740 Overland Ave., Suite C
Los Angeles, CA 90034
310-559-5833; cawso@ca.org

Co-Dependents Anonymous – If you have an excessive dependence on people, places, or things.
P.O. Box 33577
Phoenix, AZ 85067-3577; outreach@coda.org
Los Angeles CoDA
P.O. Box 90453
Los Angeles, CA 90009-0453
323-969-4995; info@lacoda.org

Codependents of Sex Addicts – If you have a family member or friend who has a problem with sexual behavior.
P.O. Box 14537
Minneapolis, MN 55414
763-537-6904; info@cosa-recovery.org

Codependents of Sex and Love Addicts Anonymous – If you have a family member or friend who has a problem with sexual behavior.
California Contact: www.coslaa.org, 860-456-0032

Compulsive Eaters Anonymous-HOW – If you have a problem with food.
5500 East Atherton St., Suite 227-B
Long Beach, CA 90815-4017
562-342-9344; gso@ceahow.org

Crystal Meth Anonymous – If you have a problem with Crystal Meth.
P.O. Box 10171
Glendale, AZ 85318-0171
www.crystalmeth.org

Debtors Anonymous – If you are addicted to money, shopping, debt, or pauperism.
P.O. Box 920888
Needham, MA 02492-0009
781-453-2743; mem@debtorsanonymous.org
Southern California Contact: www.socalda.org, 310-822-7250

Depressed Anonymous – If you have a problem with depression.
P.O. Box 17414
Louisville, KY 40217
502-569-1989; info@depressedanon.com

Dual Recovery Anonymous – If you have a problem with alcohol and/or drugs and
P.O. Box 8107 mental and/or emotional illness.
Prairie Village, Kansas 66208
877-883-2332

Eating Addictions Anonymous – If you have a problem with food.
P.O. Box 8151
Silver Spring, MD 20907-8151
202-882-6528; eaagso@eatingaddictionsanonymous.org

Emotions Anonymous – If you are habituated to any mental or emotional excess.
P.O. Box 4245
St. Paul, MN 55104-0245
651-647-9712; info@emotionsanonymous.org

Emotional Health Anonymous – If you are habituated to any mental or emotional excess.
P.O. Box 2081
San Gabriel, CA 91778
626-287-6260; sgveha@hotmail.com

Families Anonymous – If you have a family member or friend who is addicted to drugs.
P.O. Box 3475
Culver City, CA 90231-3475
800-736-9805; famanon@familiesanonymous.org

Food Addicts Anonymous – If you have a problem with food.
4623 Forest Hill Blvd., Suite #109-4
West Palm Beach, FL 33415-9120
561-967-3871; info@foodaddictsanonymous.org
Southern California Contact: 310-412-6620

Food Addicts in Recovery Anonymous – If you have a problem with food.
781-321-9118; pi@foodaddicts.org

Gam-Anon – If you have a family member or friend who has a problem with gambling or taking financial risks.
P.O. Box 157
Whitestone, NY 11357
718-352-1671; info3@gam-anon.org

Gamblers Anonymous – If you have a problem with gambling or taking financial risks.
P.O. Box 17173
Los Angeles, CA 90017
213-386-8789; isomain@gamblersanonymous.org

GreySheeters Anonymous – If you have a problem with food.
www.greysheet.org

Heroin Anonymous – If you have a problem with heroin.
livingfree@heroin-anonymous.org

Incest Survivors Anonymous – If you have a problem with incest.
P.O. Box 17245
Long Beach, CA 90807-7245
562-428-5599

Marijuana Anonymous – If you have a problem with marijuana or THC.
P.O. Box 2912
Van Nuys, CA 91404
800-766-6779; office@marijuana-anonymous.org

Methadone Anonymous – If you have a problem with methadone.
www.methadoneanonymous.info

Nar-Anon – If you have a family member or friend with a problem with narcotics.
22527 Crenshaw Blvd., #200B
Torrance, CA 90505
800-477-6291; naranonwso@hotmail.com

Narcotics Anonymous – If you have a problem with narcotics.
P.O. Box 9999
Van Nuys, CA 91404
818-773-9999; wbmail@na.org

Nicotine Anonymous – If you have a problem with nicotine.
419 Main Street, PMB#370
Huntington Beach, CA 92648
415-750-0328; info@nicotine-anonymous.org

On-Line Gamers Anonymous – If you have a problem with on-line gaming.
P.O. Box 5646
Harrisburg, PA 17110
612-245-1115; olga@olganon.org

Overeaters Anonymous – If you have a problem with food.
P.O. Box 44020
Rio Rancho, NM 87174-4020
505-891-2664; info@oa.org
Overeaters Anonymous – San Fernando Valley Intergroup Office
7133-B Darby Avenue
Reseda, CA 91335
818-881-4776

Parents Anonymous – If you have a problem with abusing your children.
675 West Foothill Blvd., Suite 220
Claremont, CA 91711-3475
909-621-6184

Rape Survivors Anonymous – If you have a problem with surviving rape.
http://groups.msn.com/RapeSurvivorsAnonymous

Recoveries Anonymous – If you seek recovery in any area.
Box 1212
East Northport, NY 11731
www.r-a.org

Recovering Couples Anonymous – If you are a couple wishing to bring recovery to your relationship.
P.O. Box 11029
Oakland, CA 94611
510-663-2312; rca_email@recovering-couples.org

S-Anon – If you have a family member or friend who has a problem with sexual behavior.
P.O. Box 111242
Nashville, TN 37222-1242
800-210-8141; sanon@sanon.org

Sex Addicts Anonymous – If you have a problem with sexual behavior.
P.O. Box 70949
Houston, TX 77270
800-477-8191; info@saa-recovery.org

Sex & Love Addicts Anonymous – If you have a problem with sexual behavior.
1550 NE Loop 410, Ste. 118
San Antonio, TX 78209
210-828-7900; info@slaafws.org
Southern California Contact: 323-957-4881, thebottomline@slaalosangeles.org

Sexaholics Anonymous – If you have a problem with sexual behavior.
P.O. Box 3565
Brentwood, TN 37024
866-424-8777; saico@sa.org
Sexaholics Anonymous Southern California Area Intergroup
P.O. Box 91083
City of Industry, CA 91715-1083
213-480-1096
www.sasocal.org

Sexual Compulsives Anonymous – If you have a problem with sexual behavior.
P.O. Box 1585, Old Chelsea Station
New York, NY 10011
800-977-4325; info@sca-recovery.org; www.sca-recovery.org
Los Angeles Contact: 310-859-5585; wsss5@yahoo.com

Smokers Anonymous – If you have a problem with tobacco smoking.
P.O. Box 84015
Los Angeles, CA 90073
310-226-7052

Social Phobics Anonymous – If you have a problem in social situations.
healsocialanxiety@hotmail.com; www.healsocialanxiety.com

Spenders Anonymous – If you have a problem with spending.
www.spenders.org

Survivors of Incest Anonymous – If you have a problem with incest.
P.O. Box 190
Benson, MD 21018-9998
410-893-3322; feedback@siawso.org

Workaholics Anonymous – If you have a problem with excessive work.
P.O. Box 289
Menlo Park, CA 94026-0289
510-273-9253; wso@workaholics-anonymous.org
Los Angeles Contact: 310-398-3710

If your 12-Step or Anonymous program is not listed and would like to be, please contact: *The 12 Steps for Everybody, P.O. Box 444, Pacific Palisades, CA 90272; call 310-428-0904, e-mail info@12stepsforeverybody.org; or visit www.12stepsforeverybody.org.*